CHOICE   MAR. '71

Religion

HITTI, Philip K. Islam; a way of life. Minnesota, 1970. 198p map
  bibl 78-104054. 6.50.   ISBN 1-8166-0569-6

Hitti, well-known as a historian of the Arabs and their culture, here
treats Islam in the context of that culture. The origins, doctrines
and practices of Islam as a religion and the history of Islam as a
state are presented in routine fashion. The section on Islam as a
culture, with chapters on science, philosophy, literature and art, is
written with more enthusiasm and imagination, but the interest, perhaps, is more in *Arab* than *Islamic* culture. The book shows some
signs of hasty composition, and contains several careless, misleading
and even inaccurate statements. Though it offers little that is not
better stated elsewhere, the book can serve the general reader as an
introduction to the culture of Arab Islam. For an introduction to
Islam as a world religion, *Mohammedanism* (2nd ed., 1962, o.p.) by
H. A. R. Gibb, remains far superior. The index is adequate; the
brief bibliography provides a good guide for beginners.

D
199.3
H67

218

Philip K. Hitti is a professor emeritus of
Semitic literature at Princeton University.
He is the author of a number of books,
among them, "History of the Arabs," "His-
tory of Syria," "Lebanon in History," and
"The Near East in History."

الاسلام : اسلوب حياة

ISLAM *A Way of Life*

PHILIP K. HITTI

ISLAM
❖ A WAY OF LIFE

University of Minnesota Press, Minneapolis

© Copyright 1970 by the University of Minnesota. All rights reserved. Printed in the United States of America at the North Central Publishing Company, St. Paul. Published in Great Britain, India, and Pakistan by the Oxford University Press, London, Bombay, and Karachi, and in Canada by the Copp Clark Publishing Co. Limited, Toronto. *Library of Congress Catalog Card Number: 78-104054.* ISBN 1-8166-0569-6

The maps on pages 6–7, 74–5, and 93 are reprinted from *Makers of Arab History*, © 1968 by Philip K. Hitti, by permission of Macmillan and Co., Ltd., St. Martin's Press, and Mr. Joseph Ascherl. The poem on pages 62–3 is reprinted from *The Mystics of Islam* by R. A. Nicholson, © 1966, by permission of Khayats, Beirut. The poem on page 60 is reprinted from *Rabi'a the Mystic and Her Fellow Saints in Islam* by Margaret Smith, © 1928, by permission of Cambridge University Press. The poems on pages 145, 147–8, and 149 are reprinted from *A Literary History of the Arabs* by R. A. Nicholson, © 1966, by permission of Cambridge University Press.

PREFACE

✤ THIS BOOK is an outgrowth of public lectures delivered to a mixed audience in spring 1967, when the author was a visiting professor on a Hill Foundation grant at the University of Minnesota, department of Middle Eastern languages. The material has since been considerably expanded and rewritten for the benefit of a reading audience. It has no claim to originality. In its compilation the author used material already worked out particularly in his *History of the Arabs* and *Makers of Arab History*.

If the reading of this volume opens a window for the reader on the rich and exciting experience of the Moslem as a man of religion, a citizen of a state, and an original thinker, and if it moves the reader to further study the subject, it will have served much of its purpose.

P. K. H.

Princeton, N.J.
April 1969

LIST OF MAPS

TABLE OF CONTENTS

Islam the Religion

Islam the State

Islam the Culture

الجزء الأوّل : الاسلام كدين

PART I *Islam the Religion*

THE PROPHET AND THE MAN

❖❖ISLAM is a way of life. As such it has three main aspects: religious, political, and cultural. The three overlap and interact, sometimes imperceptibly passing from one to the other.

Islam the religion is a system of beliefs and practices initially revealed by Allah to Muhammad, enshrined in the Arabic Koran, supplemented by tradition, and modified through the ages in response to changes in time and place. It is the third and last major monotheistic religion. A historical offshoot of Judaism and Christianity, it is most closely related to them. Originally the simple, humble religion of a few unsophisticated tribes in Arabia, Islam swelled in the course of time to become the faith of some of the most cultured peoples in medieval times. Today it has approximately four hundred and fifty million followers, who represent perhaps as many races, nationalities, and ethnic groups as any world religion. Every seventh man is a Moslem. Moslems dominate in numbers in a broad swath of land from Morocco to Pakistan and in Malaysia and Indonesia.

Islam the state is a political entity with an aggregate of institutions based on koranic law, founded by Muhammad in Medina, developed by his successors (caliphs, Ar. sing. *khalifah*) at the expense of the Persian and East Roman empires to a height unattained in medieval or ancient times, and then fragmented into splinter states in western Asia, northern Africa, and southwestern and southeastern Europe. Certain Arab and non-Arab states today style themselves Islamic.

Islam the culture is a compound of varied elements — ancient Semitic, Indo-Persian, classical Greek — synthesized under the caliphate and expressed primarily through the medium of the Arabic tongue. Unlike the other two, Islam the culture was mainly formulated by conquered peoples, Arabicized and Islamized, rather than by Arabians. It holds the distinction of having been, from the mid-eighth century to the end of the twelfth century, unmatched in its brilliancy and unsurpassed in its literary, scientific, and philosophic output.

I

IT ALL started with one man. The name given that man by his parents remains uncertain. The one by which he is generally known, Muhammad ("highly praised"), sounds like an honorary title. Hardly anyone before him bore that name. In his youth he was known to his people as al-Amin ("the trustworthy").

The name of the city of Muhammad's birth in 570, Makkah (Mecca), has become well known thanks to the hundreds of thousands of his followers who through the ages have annually flocked to its shrine. Yathrib, the city of his burial, has been designated al-Madinah (Medina), "the city," and shares with its sister Mecca the interest of the annual pilgrims. The year of Muhammad's migration (*hijrah*, Hegira, A.D. 610) from the city of his nativity to the city of his missionary activity has become the starting date of the Moslem calendar. Hijaz, the region in which he was born, had never figured prominently on a national or an international level, but it became and has remained a holy land for a sizable segment of mankind. In fact at the time of Muhammad's birth the entire Arabian peninsula — heathen, tribal, and a desolate area on the map — was in eclipse; the limelight glittered with full brilliancy over the Byzantine area to the northwest and the Persian area to the northeast. The book for which Muhammad was responsible shares with the Bible the distinction of being one of the two most widely read books, the only two perennial best sellers.

Though some historic facts about Muhammad are known, Muhammad the man eludes us. The earliest reference to him is a seventh-century passing one in Syriac, the language used by the common people of the Fertile Crescent to the north. In Greek, the lingua franca of the Fertile Crescent, the first mention of the "ruler of the Saracens and the pseudo-prophet" occurs in a chronicle written two hundred years after his death. The earliest Arabic biography was written by one who died in Baghdad a hundred and forty years after Muhammad's death; it has survived in a recension by ibn-Hisham, who died in al-Fustat (Old Cairo) in 833. By then the historical man had become a legendary figure, an archetype of the perfect man. In all the literature about him the historical is inextricably mixed with the legendary, and the halo of sanctity around the Prophet's head is forever fixed. The admiration of his followers for their national hero, founder of their faith, initiator of their state, creator of their glory, passed from idealization to idolization.

The first glimpse of Muhammad offered by history is of an orphan child born to an impoverished family, a fact corroborated in an early chapter (surah, 93:6–7) of the Koran. This book provides the best source of facts about his life. Muhammad's father died on a caravan journey to Syria before the child's birth. His mother died when he was about six years old. The grandfather who took charge of him died two years later leaving the troubled child in the custody of his uncle abu-Talib. The clan into which Muhammad was born, the banu-Hashim ("children of Hashim"), had fallen on bad times and did not share with its tribe, the Quraysh, the prosperity that tribe enjoyed and the power it possessed.

Years pass before history records a second glimpse of Muhammad. He is by then twenty-five years old, married to his employer, a wealthy Qurayshite widow who was then forty. Her business involved trade and caravans, the most lucrative commerce of the day. For the first time in his life Muhammad had sufficient income, a fact of such importance that it was cited in the Koran (93:4–5, 8).

Mecca was then the scene of a radical socioeconomic change involving the transition from a partly Bedouin to an urban society. It was on its way to becoming the capital of the area. Its leading tribe, the Quraysh, was becoming mercantile as a result of the control it exercised on the caravans. The city lay on the crossroads of trade routes

4

between the frankincense and spice lands of Yaman and the Mediterranean seaports to the north. It owed its site to the Zamzam, a well that was brackish but still attractive to desert caravans. The sensitive would-be social reformer must have noted with concern the widening gap between the settled, wealthier people and the poorer nomads. He had himself experienced both ends of the economic spectrum.

The tribal transition, as in the case of the national transition, involved psychological tensions. Traditional loyalties were strained and old values downgraded. Tribal solidarity — basic for survival in desert life — and physical courage — a prerequisite for prestige and leadership in a nomadic society — give way in a capitalistic society to individual initiative, industry, and wealth. The tension in loyalties must have involved religious ones throughout the area as indicated by the mushrooming of a crop of "prophets" in different parts of the peninsula.

In the performance of his new duties the future prophet must have had personal contacts with Syrian and Abyssinian Christian merchants, travelers, and slaves. Besides, there was an ancient Christian community in Najran, on the southern border of Hijaz, and two Christianized Arabian tribes on the northeast and northwest margins of the peninsula. This means there were Christian Arabs before Moslem Arabs. Then there were Arabicized Jewish tribes in and near Medina. From such sources Muhammad must have gained the impression that while Christians and Jews had each a "book" (scripture) and were more advanced, his people had no book and lagged behind.

The third historical snapshot of the man showed him to be moody and distraught. The year was 610. Torn between doubts and aspirations he indulged in retreats while seeking a solution for the obsessing problem of what to do about the lag between his people and the Christians and Jews. On one of these occasions, while contemplating in his favorite hill cave outside of Mecca, he heard a voice exhorting him:

> Recite, in the name of thy Lord, who created,
> Created man from a clot of blood.

And as if the confused man questioned his ability to recite, the voice continued:

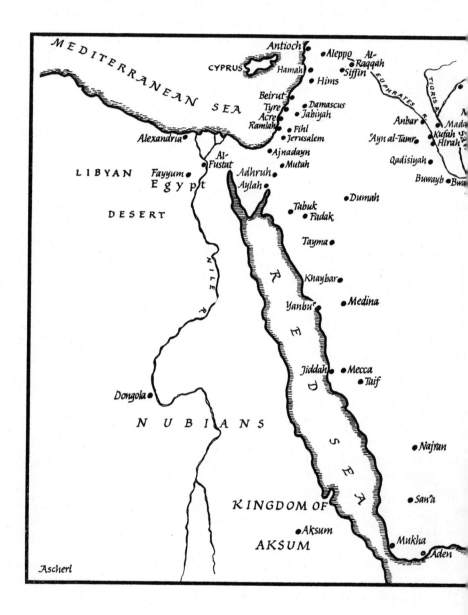

The Arabian Peninsula at the Time of Muhammad, ca. 600

Recite, for thy Lord is the most bounteous,
Who teacheth by the pen,
Teacheth man what he did not know.

(96:1–5)

After a brief interval the voice came again like the "reverberating of bells." Muhammad must have been in a state of ecstasy accompanied by chills, for he rushed home and asked his wife to put more covers on him. As if in a trance he then heard:

O thou, enwrapped in thy mantle,
Arise and warn!

(74:1–2)

No more doubt about it, the voice was that of an angel, later identified as Gabriel. And so the Prophet was born. The day is still commemorated throughout the world of Islam, usually on the twenty-seventh of Ramadan. (A holy period in pre-Islam, Ramadan is the only month mentioned in the Koran [2:181].) A surah (97) is dedicated to the episode. In its introduction the entire revelation of the Koran, which was recorded over a period of twenty-two years, is telescoped in one vision, in one night: "Lo, We have sent it down on the night of power." That night is further described as more worthy than "a thousand months."

II

ISLAM shares with Judaism and Christianity the concept of revelation, but in a different form. The concept is prompted by man's feeling of insecurity and inability to cope with the besetting problems of life and his desire for guidance and support from a supreme source. More than inspiration in the Christian sense, as the process by which the divine mind works through human consciousness, the Moslem view of revelation (*wahy*) is tantamount to dictation. Word form and contents are God's. The process is described as "sending down," down from heaven where lay an archetype. It entails a passive recipient to whom God communicates his thought and will. When thus commissioned, the recipient is "sent forth" to announce the message. He becomes God's messenger. Accordingly Allah, on one of several occasions, commissioned Muhammad:

8

We have given revelation to thee just as We gave revelation to
Noah and the prophets after him. We also gave revelation to
Abraham, to Ishmael, to Isaac, to Jacob, to the Tribes [pa-
triarchs descended from Jacob], to Jesus, to Job, to Jonah, to
Aaron, and to Solomon; while to David We gave a Psalter
[*zabur*, from Heb. *mizmor*].

(4:161-2)

There were also messengers whose stories We have told thee before, and messengers whose stories We have not told thee.

To each people God sends one messenger (10:48; 16:38; cf.
23:46). In each case the messenger is entrusted with a book, con-
firmatory of the preceding books. Muhammad was sent to a people
lacking a book, a people to whom God had not yet sent a messenger.
The Koran is revealed in Arabic, and Arabic thus became an integral
part of the revelation. Arabs refer to it as "the tongue of the angels,"
meaning, in the opinion of one struggling to learn it, no one can master
it until he dies and becomes an angel. Additionally, Arabic, the language of the Koran, served as a basis for a new nation to be created by
Muhammad from motley, unruly Arabian tribes that had never united
before. Thus, the founder of Islam added a new dimension to his triple
contribution of religion, state, and culture.

Lo, We have made it an Arabic Koran, so that ye may understand
And lo, it is in the Mother of the Book [the heavenly archetype]
in Our presence, exalted, wise.

(43:2-3)

Again and again the divine nature of the Koran is emphasized and
Muhammad is ordered to proclaim nothing but what is revealed (43:42).
Meantime the messenger's audience is duly notified:

Thus have We sent to you a messenger from amongst yourselves
to recite to you Our revelation, to purify you and to instruct you
in the book and the wisdom and to teach you what ye do not
know.

(2:146)

And as if eager to remove all possibility of misunderstanding, Allah
adds: "And Muhammad is naught but a messenger" (3:138).

Messengership was a Christian concept that had been institution-
alized for centuries. Jesus "sent forth" his twelve disciples, who became apostles, or envoys. An apostle was one sent by God. The title

9

was later applied to other than disciples, like Paul, who carried on the message. The Koran bestows on Muhammad another title — "prophet." In several verses he is commissioned as a prophet and is so addressed by Allah:

> O prophet, We have sent thee as a witness, a bringer
> of good tidings and a warner,
> A summoner to Allah by His permission and a
> light-giving lamp.
>
> (33:44–5)

In another surah the prophet is characterized as *ummi*.

> Say: "O mankind, I am Allah's messenger to you all,
> Of Him to whom belongeth the kingdom of the heavens
> and of the earth.
>
> There is no god but He.
> He giveth life and causeth to die.
> Believe then in Allah and in His messenger,
> The *ummi* prophet, who himself believeth in Allah
> and His words, and follow him;
> Haply so ye will be guided."
>
> (7:157–8; cf. 7:156)

Moslem commentators are in agreement that *ummi* means "unlettered," or "illiterate." Modern scholars, however, argue that Muhammad, as one engaged in trade, could probably read and write, and that the term, judged by the context, probably means one belonging to a community without a book and therefore uninstructed in scriptures (cf. 3:19).

The Arabic word for "prophet" (*nabi*) is the same as in Aramaic and Hebrew, indicating its Semitic origin. It had a long history before its koranic use, but it does not occur in pre-Islamic literature. It figured prominently in the Old Testament story of Samuel (1 Sam. 10:5), a thousand years before Christ. Even earlier Deborah is styled a prophetess and a judge (Judg. 4:4). The Old Testament records cases of a long chain of men — all chosen and addressed by God — from Moses (Exod. 3:2 et seq.) through Samuel (1 Sam. 3:3 et seq.) and Jeremiah (Jer. 1:4–10) to Ezekiel (Ezek. 1:1 et seq.) and Zechariah (Zech. 1:7 et seq.). Sixteen books of the Old Testament were written by prophets. All prophets were illuminated expounders of revelation. To them the word of God came in a variety of ways with the command that they should proclaim it. Some were oral prophets whose discourses were never committed into writing. The concern of the early prophets with law and the rules employed in executing the law gave way in the later ones to concern with ethical monotheism and its propagation.

The prophets enumerated in the Koran are largely Old Testament characters. Among them Abraham stands out as Muhammad's favorite. Besides having one surah (14) dedicated to him, he is mentioned about seventy-five times in twenty-five different surahs. Of the New Testament characters only four are given clear mention: Zacharias, John the Baptist, Jesus, and Mary. The Koran adds Muhammad to this biblical list and thereby legitimizes his prophethood.

But while the Moslem Prophet comes chronologically at the bottom of this long and honorable list, in significance he is ranked at the top. He is the "seal [khatam] of the prophets" (33:40), the last to be charged by God. His dispensation sums up and supplements all preceding ones; eventually it supplants them all. The abrogation of the older revelations was necessitated by their "falsification" by Jews and Christians. Muhammad is reported to have said repeatedly "no prophet after me." Through Muhammad God sent his final word to mankind. No one can thereafter improve on it.

III

CONSECRATED and fired by the new task assigned him, the Messenger-Prophet began with his own people. He taught, preached, and admonished as he delivered the new message. It was initially as clear as it was simple. There is only one God, Allah. He is all-powerful, the creator of all, the everlasting. There is a paradise and there is a hell. Splendid rewards await those who obey His commands. Terrible punishment awaits those who disregard them. Disappointed with the lack of receptivity to his message, the teacher-preacher turned to warning people that the day of judgment was imminent. But his was another voice in the wilderness. Neither fear nor reward proved to be an effective motivator.

The Allah he preached about was not new to Meccans. Indeed He was the principal deity of a group enshrined in their al-Ka'bah (Kaabah), the leading sanctuary of Hijaz. The objection was not to him as such but to this exclusiveness required in worshiping him. Acceptance of the new doctrine would eliminate all other deities and would thereby alienate the people from their fathers, who worshiped many deities. Besides, the new teaching would consign all those fathers to hell. The Quraysh — particularly its Umayyad clan — custodians of the Kaabah and the Zamzam, controllers of the caravan trade, and oligarchic masters of the city, had special reasons for resistance. The new preaching might jeopardize pilgrimages to the Kaabah, next to trade their main source of income. Moreover, the once-poor orphan was introducing such dangerous economic doctrines as the rightful claim of beggars and the destitute to a share in the wealth of the rich (70:24–5). Additionally he advocated a dangerous doctrine, one that would substitute faith for blood as the social bond of community life. If "the believers are naught but brothers" (49:10) was acted upon, the entire family, clan, and tribal unity would be undermined and replaced by religious unity. Then there were dangerous political implications in Muhammad's teaching. Religious success could entail political success, and the new prophet was a potential new ruler. Shrewd merchants that they were, they found nothing in what he offered that they cared to buy.

The opposition at first did not take the upstart seriously. Silence was followed by verbal attacks. He was "possessed by jinn" (81:22) said some; no, he was "a falsifying magician" (38:3) claimed others; "a soothsayer" (69:42) asserted still others. In this discouraging debut on the stage of prophethood, Muhammad was sustained and encouraged by his first convert, his wife Khadijah. As long as she lived, he had no other wife. His cousin 'Ali, son of abu-Talib in whose house he was brought up, was probably his second convert. Another early and valuable recruit from the Quraysh was abu-Bakr, the future father-in-law and first successor of the Prophet. But the bulk of followers were from the lowest classes — the poor and the slaves — the "meanest" in the koranic phrase (26:111).

At last the time came for the aristocracy of his tribe, the banu-Umayyah, to engage in active persecution. This necessitated the migration (in 615) of eighty-three families of his followers to Christian

Abyssinia, considered safe because its people believed in one God. But Muhammad himself held out. His patron abu-Talib refused to deliver him to his enemies because the clannish code of honor so dictated. A new weapon was devised: economic and social boycott. A quarantine was imposed on the recalcitrant clan. For three years the entire tribe refused to deal with members of Muhammad's clan. Toward the end of this period (619) both Muhammad's noble-minded wife Khadijah and his chivalrous uncle died.

Muhammad's position as a prophet was deteriorating, despite the addition of a few fresh recruits. Outstanding among them was another Qurayshite, 'Umar ibn-al-Khattab, who was to become another of Muhammad's successors as well as his father-in-law. The core of the opposition, the Umayyads, remained adamant in its hostility. Muhammad felt it necessary to seek a new field for his missionary activity. Taif, a fertile settlement on a high plateau seventy-five miles southeast of Mecca, was chosen. But the move, to use an Arabic figure of speech, was from under the leak to under the main. The city was a favorite summer resort for rich Meccans. It housed a shrine for the exalted goddess Allat. But the Lady of Taif was not ready for dethronement, and the intruder's teaching ran counter to other established interests here no less than in Mecca. The town gave its guest a rude welcome. A mob flung stones at him. The garden in which he sought refuge offered no refuge; it was owned by a leader of the opposition. The expatriate had to return from where he came. No other course seemed open. Dejected, he turned his back on Taif and faced Mecca, the city that had earlier rejected him, with the following moving Davidian prayer on his lips:

> O Lord, unto Thee do I complain of my helplessness, paucity of resourcefulness and insignificance vis-à-vis other men. O most merciful of the merciful, Thou art the lord of the helpless and Thou art my lord. To whom wilt Thou abandon me? To one who would abuse me? Or to one who has been given power over me? Assuredly if Thy wrath is not upon me, I have no worry. For Thy favor then encompasseth me. I therefore seek refuge in the light of Thy countenance, the light by which darkness is illumined and all affairs of this world and the world to come are rightly ordered. May it never

be that I should incur Thy anger or fail to satisfy Thee. For there is no resource and no power save in Thee.[1]

The second period of residence in Mecca was productive of no better results than the first, but occasional visits to the annual fairs held in the city opened up new prospects. These fairs attracted pilgrims to the great sanctuary as well as buyers and sellers from neighboring desert camps and settlements. They also provided opportunities for competitive poetical contests. On one of his visits Muhammad got acquainted with a group from Yathrib, two hundred and fifty miles north, who seemed to be mildly interested in him. Perhaps they thought Muhammad was the great religious leader their Jewish fellow townsmen were expecting to appear. Muhammad's negotiations with a delegation of seventy-two representatives of Yathrib resulted in an invitation and a guarantee of security and protection for the guest and his followers.

To escape the Umayyad vigilance Muhammad had about two hundred of his followers slip quietly out of Mecca. Accompanied by 'Ali and abu-Bakr, Muhammad followed and arrived on September 24, 622. In 639 the second caliph, 'Umar ibn-al-Khattab, fixed this hijrah date — he, however, made it begin with July 16, 622 — rather than the birth date, as the starting point of the new calendar. With this migration (hijrah, wrongly translated as "flight") one period — the Meccan — ended and another — the Medinese — began.

More than that the hijrah marks the end of the pre-Islamic era and the start of the Islamic. For Muhammad it was the point in his career when he turned from a pattern of frustration to self-realization. The city would no more be known as Yathrib; it became "the city [of the Prophet]," al-Madinah. The Muhajirun ("Emigrants") became a distinct group, the vanguard of Islam. A handful of them, as later chapters will show, constituted a living link between Muhammad and what became Muhammadanism. Those of Medina who embraced the new faith were also recognized, and they were called the Ansar ("Supporters"). The two groups became known as the Sahabah ("Companions"), the elite and future nobility of the new community-state.

---

[1] Ibn-Hisham, *Sirah*, ed. Ferdinand Wüstenfeld (Gottingen, 1858–9), p. 280; cf. Alfred Guillaume, tr., *The Life of Muhammad* (London, 1955), p. 193.

14

In Medina Muhammad's writings centered more on social and political matters than on spiritual considerations. The short, crisp, spiritually oriented revelations that he made in Mecca were followed by prosaic, verbose surahs revealed in Medina and dealing with such subjects as war and booty, gambling and taxes, food and drink, and marriage and divorce. The community of Medina served as the nucleus of the rising Arab nation; its government developed into a prototype of the Moslem empire, and the Islam of Medina was the germ from which the Islam of the world grew.

The milieu in which Islam grew differed radically from that in which it was born. The Medinese society was agricultural rather than commercial. The structure of its population was a composite of two powerful tribes competing for ascendancy and three minor tribes whose members were adherents of Judaism. The city lacked the unified leadership and control exercised in Mecca by the Umayyads. This played in favor of a forthcoming leader. Otherwise, the malaise from which both cities suffered was basically the same. The Medinese community was in a state of transition, passing from a nomadic to an urban culture, with the concomitant dislocation in the economic, social, and psychological structures.

For the newcomers the first two years were especially difficult. They had problems obtaining food and housing and adjusting to a new environment. The immediate solution lay in having each newly converted family extend full hospitality to an emigrant family. Thereby the proclaimed theory that the new religion was a fraternal order was put into practice. But the economic condition of Medina was getting progressively worse. New sources of revenue had to be discovered. Meccan caravans returning from Syria with cash and goods offered an easy target as well as a chance to injure the lifeline of Mecca.

The first raid was well timed and well located. It occurred during Ramadan (mid-March 624), one of the four "sacred months" (9:36) in which warring was prohibited except in self-defense. The location was a watering place southwest of Medina, named Badr, at which the next caravan was sure to stop. The caravan numbered a thousand camels; Muhammad, according to ibn-Hisham, could muster only 312 men.

15

The caravan leader and Umayyad chief, abu-Sufyan, had got wind of the contemplated attack and sent for aid from Mecca. His reinforcement included nine hundred men, accompanied by female singers to spark the fighters' enthusiasm. Following the usual procedure the combat began with single challenges between champions. Confident of victory the Quraysh fought with no plan and under no discipline. The attackers were given instructions about formation and method by their leader. They fought for survival and Allah; the will to conquer was on their side. The foe fought for its possessions and was routed, losing seventy dead and seventy prisoners. The Moslems lost fourteen men, the first martyrs to the cause of Allah. Against the advice of 'Umar ibn-al-Khattab and other sanguinary men, ransom was accepted. It was more useful than bloodshed.

There could be no question about it: the feat was accomplished with divine support. In fact the Koran (9:9–12, 17) gives the exact number of angels, a thousand, sent to participate in the battle. The first encounter between monotheism and polytheism ended in victory, a divine sanction of the new faith. Badr, distinguished by a mention in the Koran (3:119), became the source of inspiration for future wars. In the distribution of the booty God and his Messenger received one fifth (8:42); that set a precedent for future conquests.

The defeat was humiliating to the Meccans but not annihilating. Twelve months later the same foe, led by the same man, was again ready to measure swords. The encounter took place at Uhud on the side of the valley opposite Medina. Abu-Sufyan scored a victory. During the battle a stone hit the Prophet, and when he fell he smashed a tooth and cut his lip. But the victory was not enough to tarnish the glamour of Badr, and both sides expected a final round.

It came. Muhammad could muster only three thousand troops. In 627 at the head of a coalition of Meccans, mercenary Bedouins, black slaves, and allied Jews — ten thousand in all — abu-Sufyan moved against Medina and found it defended by a series of trenches, an innovation in Arabian warfare suggested by a Persian follower of Muhammad. The effect of the innovation must have been as demoralizing as the introduction of the tank was in World War I. The trench rendered the six hundred cavalrymen ineffective. Especially disgusted were the Bedouins, whose main interest in fighting was pay and booty. The loosely held confederation began to fall apart. The encounter was a match between number and wits. Moslem leadership was not only more intelligent, it also had a better intelligence agency. After a month's siege the invaders withdrew, leaving twenty dead, and never again challenged Islam. The battle, commemorated in the Koran by surah 33 ("The Confederates") is commonly styled that of the "trench" (*khandaq*).

The way was now open for Moslem hegemony in the area. The Quraysh lost not only their prestige, but their hold on the trade route to Syria as well. Throughout his Meccan period Muhammad had acted on the assumption that his religion was ideologically so closely related to the two older monotheisms — particularly Judaism — that there could be no difficulty in establishing it organically within their framework (2:127-31). Abraham's religion was the mother of Islam, and Abraham himself was the father of the Arabians through Hagar and Ishmael. It was he who rebuilt and purified the Kaabah as the "house [*bayt*] of Allah" (2:119) after its destruction by the Deluge. The women of the "people of the book" were made legitimate as wives to Moslems, and their food was also legitimized (5:7). Muhammad's harem included a Christian (Mariyah) and a Jewish wife. He prayed toward Jerusalem and his followers were ordered to do so. It was not long, however, after his landing at Medina that he began to be disillusioned. The Jews, he came to realize, considered themselves God's chosen people, the only seed of Abraham; they neither accepted others into Judaism nor themselves left it in favor of other religions. The expected Messiah could rise from no other tribe but theirs.

However, the break with the Jews had an economic aspect as well as a religious one. Early in the second year at Medina the mounting need for rehabilitating the expatriates was augmented by military preparations. Muhammad expected his Jewish neighbors, as quasi-brothers of Moslems, to contribute freely to the community chest. But a unilateral brotherhood is no brotherhood, and since they did not agree to Muhammad's request they were denounced in several koranic passages. The cold war that ensued was bound to lead to a hot war. A silly trick by a Jewish merchant on a Moslem woman customer

17

sparked the conflict. Those of the Jewish tribe who survived found refuge in Syria. The weapons and other possessions they left behind supplied a much needed relief to the Moslems. The next year (625) saw the expulsion of the second tribe of Jews. Their houses and palm gardens were no less welcome than the possessions of the first tribe. The Moslems next turned (in 628) against Khaybar, a fertile Jewish oasis a hundred miles north of Medina. Khaybar had served as an asylum for exiled Medinese Jews and as a source of that contingent of Jews which took part in the "battle of the trench." Its defenses against Bedouin attacks rendered it, in the eyes of its inhabitants, impregnable. But the forthcoming was not a Bedouin attack, and it took only two weeks to force a surrender. The terms included the annual delivery of one half of the yield of the oasis' gardens and fields. The Jewish problem of Arabia was thus solved.

In the meantime a movement to Islamize the religious practices that had been borrowed from Judaism was under way. The direction of the ritual prayer (kiblah, Ar. *qiblah*) was changed from Jerusalem to Mecca (2:139, 144-5). The human voice calling for prayer replaced the trumpet and the gong used by Jews and Christians. It was certainly a more effective means. Friday was ordained as the only day for congregational prayer (62:9-11). That day (*Jum'ah*, "assembly day") was chosen because it was the weekly shopping day when Jews particularly flocked to the market to buy provisions for their Sabbath. Once begun, the Arabization, the nationalization of Islam, continued. Ramadan was fixed as a month of fasting. Pilgrimage to the Kaabah was authorized and the kissing of the Black Stone — a pre-Islamic fetish housed in the Kaabah's corner — was sanctioned. In the pilgrimage Islam accepted its richest heritage from polytheistic Arabia and thereby alienated itself further from its two historic sisters.

While Islam was in its formative state Muhammad lacked the opportunity of establishing firsthand contact with a Christian community comparable to that established with the Jewish — hence the preponderant Jewish imprint on his religion. His contacts with Christians were limited to personal contacts with a few Christian individuals. Besides a Christian (Coptic) concubine, he had a Christian (Abyssinian) ex-slave and a Christian adopted son, Zayd. Besides the his-

18

toric contacts with Christians, there is a Moslem legend that Muhammad had for a teacher a Syrian monk, Bahira, whom young Muhammad met when on a caravan to Damascus. The nearest Arabian Christian communities were on the southern border of Hijaz (Najranites), the northeastern border of Syria (Ghassanids), and the northwestern frontier of Persia (Lakhmids). All three communities belonged to the Syrian Church, whose views on the nature of Christ and the relation of his humanity to his divinity were considered equally heretical by both Catholic and Orthodox churches. Even so, no Christian Arabic texts were available to Muhammad, and his sources of information were oral and secondhand with an inextricable mixture of biblical and pseudo-biblical material. The Gospels (*Injil*, from Gr. *Evangel*) are mentioned eleven times in five different surahs, but there is no reference to Paul or the Epistles. In principle the Koran takes the position of confirming and rectifying the Christian Scriptures; in practice it abrogates them.

Of the four New Testament characters known to Muhammad, Jesus ('Isa) stands out as the most prominent. In fact he holds the distinction among all other prophets in his supernatural birth (3:40 et seq.) — that is, being the Messiah and the "word of God" (cf. John 1:1) — and in his being a "spirit from God" (4:169). Jesus's commission takes the form of an enabling act. "And to Jesus, son of Mary, gave We clear proofs of his mission and strengthened him with that spirit of holiness" (2:81). The proofs are the miracles he performed. Not only does Jesus heal the sick but he performs miracles while in the cradle (3:41, 43; 5:110), which echoes an apocryphal story in the Gospel of Infancy of which a Coptic copy is extant. But Jesus was neither killed nor crucified (4:155). He was "lifted up to God." When it comes to functioning, though, Christ is no different from any other prophet.

What irked Muhammad in particular were the dogma of the Trinity and its related doctrine of incarnation as he understood them. A belief in three Gods collided head on with his basic dogma of the oneness of God. The sonship of Christ aided and comforted his Meccan enemies, who believed Allah had sons and daughters. Several koranic passages were intended to refute the Christian doctrine. "Say not

19

'three' . . . Allah is only one god" (4:169); "They surely are infidels who say 'Allah is the third of three'" (5:77); "Far be it from Him that He should have a son" (4:177); "He neither begets nor is begotten" (112:3); "O Jesus, son of Mary, hast thou said unto mankind, 'Take me and my mother as two gods beside God?'" (5:116). Jesus and Mary are often associated in koranic passages. Mary acquires a super-human feature and is made the daughter of 'Imran and sister of Aaron (19:16–29; 3:31–40). But on the whole Muhammad's attitude remained more sympathetic toward Christians than toward Jews. He fought no battles with the Christians. In one surah (5:85) Jews and idolaters are made the most vehement in hostility, whereas Christians are considered as nearest in affection.

When in 630 a Najran Christian delegation presented itself freely, and with no preceding hostility, to pay homage to Muhammad, it received favorable consideration. In return for a specified amount of taxes and a variety of services the people of Najran were granted a treaty, a copy of which has been preserved by an early historian of the conquests:

> They are entitled to the protection of Allah and the security of Muhammad the Prophet, the Messenger of Allah, which security shall involve their persons, religion, lands and possessions — including those of them who are absent as well as those who are present — their camels, messengers and images [church pictures and crosses]. The status they previously held shall not be changed, nor shall any of their religious services or images be altered. No attempt shall be made to turn a bishop from his office as a bishop; a monk from his office as a monk, nor a sexton of a church from his office, whether what is under the control of each is great or small. These Christians shall not be held responsible for any wrong deed or bloodshed in pre-Islamic time. They shall neither be called to military service nor compelled to pay the tithe.[2]

Shortly before the subjugation of Khaybar, Muhammad conceived the brilliant idea of undertaking, at the head of a band of followers, a holy pilgrimage to Mecca in the hope of convincing its people that there was a place in his scheme for their sanctuary and its associated institution. But the Quraysh, learning that he was leading fifteen hundred men, put a different interpretation on the move. With two hun-

[2] Al-Baladhuri, *Origins of the Islamic State (Kitab Futuh al-Buldan)*, tr. Philip K. Hitti (New York, 1916; reprint Beirut, 1966), pp. 100–1.

dred cavalry they went out ready to battle the invaders. At al-Hudaybiyah (nine miles north of Mecca) the two parties met. Messengers shuttled back and forth. After some bargaining a pact of nonaggression was signed, providing for cessation of hostility and future coexistence. Muhammad returned to Medina after scoring this significant peaceful victory. He could now, with no fear from an enemy at his back, proceed to consolidate what he had, expand it, and extend his Pax Islamica over it. In the two years following he sent bands led by his lieutenants on more than a dozen expeditions against tribes and settlements in the north as far as southern Palestine. The farthest point reached was Mu'tah near the southern end of the Dead Sea. We are not told what the objective was, but presumably it was to secure full control of the trade route, which had remained idle since the Badr episode, and to establish contact with Arabians long domiciled in Syria. Treaties of peace were signed with several Christian and Jewish settlements, putting them under the protection of the newly rising religio-political power in consideration of a tribute payment (*jizyah*). A precedent far-reaching in its consequences was set.

Moslem historians would have us believe that in this period the Prophet sent messages to neighboring heads of state — including the Byzantine and Persian — summoning them to Islam. The supposed texts of some of these messages have even been reproduced. However, it is difficult to accept the idea that a self-proclaimed prophet who had not yet been generally recognized by his own people should think in those terms.

Events moved quickly to a climax. The long-awaited hour came. In January 630 Muhammad, backed by a thousand followers, made his triumphal entry into the city of his birth. Realizing the futility of any further opposition the Quraysh yielded. Even abu-Sufyan, the arch-enemy of Islam, was ready to embrace the faith he had fought violently for so long. Before this time two other Qurayshites, Khalid ibn-al-Walid and 'Amr ibn-al-'As, had been recruited to the cause. Against the advice of 'Umar ibn-al-Khattab and other aides, the victor proscribed only ten of the opposition leaders. Abu-Sufyan was spared. Such self-restraint and statesmanship have few parallels in the annals of that time. Muhammad, predictably, lost no time in making his way into the Kaabah, there to smash the three hundred and sixty idols while exclaiming, "Truth hath come, and falsehood hath vanished!"

Some historians assure us that in this year, the "year of delegations," delegations from all over the peninsula — from as far as Hadramawt, 'Uman, and Bahrayn — rushed to offer homage to the prince-prophet together with the prescribed alms (*zakah*). Considering the existent means of communication, this must be regarded as one of those cases where events are viewed in the light of future developments. How could the Arabian grapevine, uncanny as it was, have flashed the word and translated it into action over thousands of miles in so short a time?

In spring 632 the sixty-two-year-old chief led a large body of believers to undertake the annual pilgrimage to Mecca. After going through the rites prescribed in the Koran, he delivered one of the noblest sermons of his career. It began:

> Harken, O ye men, unto my words and take ye them to heart. Know ye that every Moslem is a brother unto every other Moslem, and that ye are now one brotherhood [cf. sur. 49:10]. It is, therefore, not legitimate for any one of you to appropriate unto himself anything that belongs to his brother unless it is willingly given by that brother.[3]

Substituting the religious for the centuries-old blood bond as the basis for social cohesion was, indeed, a daring and original accomplishment of the Prophet of Arabia.

Three months later, on June 8, 632, Muhammad took ill in his home at Medina and died complaining of severe headache. He was buried under the floor of the mud hut of his favorite wife, 'A'ishah.

IV

CHRISTIANS of medieval times misunderstood Muhammad and considered him a despicable character. The reasons, as will be shown later, were more historical — that is, economic and political — than ideological. His earliest portrait as a false prophet and imposter, sketched by a ninth-century Greek chronicler, was later embellished with the bright

[3] Ibn-Hisham, *Sirah* (Cairo, 1929), p. 26. Cf. Philip K. Hitti, *History of the Arabs*, 10th ed. (London and New York, 1970), p. 120.

colors of oversexuality, dissoluteness, bloodthirstiness, and brigandage. In clerical circles Muhammad became the antichrist. His dead body was suspended somewhere between heaven and earth until an Italian convert in 1503 visited Medina and was evidently surprised not to find it in that position. Dante bisected the trunk of Muhammad's body and consigned it to the ninth hell as befits the chief of the damned souls, bringers of schism into religion.

Western fablers used Maumet — one of forty-one variants of Muhammad's name listed in the *Oxford English Dictionary* — in the sense of idol. It came to mean "puppet" or "doll." In this sense Shakespeare used the word in *Romeo and Juliet*. Another variant of the same name, Mahoun, was used in English medieval encyclical plays as an object of worship. Ironically the greatest iconoclast and the leading champion of the oneness of God in history was metamorphosed into an object of worship.

The Prophet's followers magnified his strong points, while others denied them. Neither he nor the Koran ever claimed that he was anything but a man, with no superhuman quality, but believers lifted him above mankind, endowed him with miracle-working power, and, in folk religion, surrounded him with an aura of sanctity.

But the founder of Islam cannot be equated with the founder of Christianity. Muhammad had no unusual intrinsic quality and possessed no special authority; he was simply the vehicle for transmitting God's word. To that extent he corresponds to the Virgin Mary. This, it should be remembered, is the learned belief as distinguished from folk belief. Moslems, therefore, object to being designated Muhammadans as a parallel to the designation of Christians. Those modern Orientalists who still use freely the objectionable term should know better than to call people by names they don't like. "Moslem" (Muslim) literally is one who surrenders himself (to the will of God). Islam, therefore, is not the religion of Muhammad, but the religion of surrender to God's will. The surrender implicit in the submission of Abraham and his son in the supreme test — the attempted sacrifice expressed in the word *aslama* (37:103) — was evidently the act that prompted Muhammad's use of the name for the new faith.

Among modern writers there are those who have endeavored to

debunk the hero or psychoanalyze the husband, thereby adding pseudo-scientific judgments to the mass of prejudiced and legendary opinions. The visionary trances he experienced, we are assured, were no more than epileptic fits. (Not far from Princeton flourishes an epileptic colony, but no one there has qualified so far as a prophet.) As long as the husband was satisfied (so we are told) with one wife, Khadijah, his sex urge was sublimated and his contribution considerable, but once he overstocked his harem, the man deteriorated in character. The "deterioration," in the eyes of his believers, was no more than adaptation to the requirements of a new situation.

In fact Muhammad's character is portrayed with greater fidelity in the Koran than in any other source. The battles he fought, the judgments he made, and the feats he accomplished leave no doubt about his endowment with a strong personality, deep convictions, dedication, and other qualities that make leaders of men. He, once a poor orphan, always had a place in his heart for the underprivileged:

> Therefore the orphan oppress not
> And the beggar drive not away.   (93:9–10)

In a weak moment he acknowledged the three mighty Meccan goddesses (Allat, al-'Uzza, and Manah) as intercessors with Allah, only to withdraw that recognition shortly afterward (53:19–23). The temptation was attributed to Satan (22:51–2). In another weak moment he contracted a prohibited marriage with the wife of his adopted son Zayd and proceeded to justify it by revelation (33:37). The revelation authorized four wives (4:3), but by some "prophetic privilege" he added five others, considering them as honorary wives. Some, no doubt, were taken into the harem for political or other nonconjugal purposes.

Judged only by achievement, Muhammad the man, the teacher, the orator, the author, the statesman, and the warrior stands out as one of the ablest men in all history. He laid the basis of a religion — Islam; initiated a state — the caliphate; prompted a culture — the Arabic-Islamic culture; and founded a nation — the Arab nation. He is still a living force in the lives of millions of men.

THE BOOK: BELIEFS AND PRACTICES

◆◆◆ FEW PEOPLES in history seem to have been as susceptible to the
influence of the word, spoken or written, as the "sons of Arabic,"
the Arabs' favorite designation of themselves. It was only in the field
of verbal expression that pre-Islamic Arabians distinguished themselves. The extent to which they developed their language is surprising; it was out of proportion to the development of their political, social, and economic institutions. How illiterate camel breeders living in
scattered tribes, with no political cohesion to unite them, could develop a refined, richly worded means of expression remains a mystery.

Linguistic development culminated in rhythmical, usually metri-
cal, composition known as rhymed prose, or poetry. The ability to cre-
ate such composition was the Bedouins' only cultural asset. Typical
Semites, those early Arabians neither created nor promoted any art
other than the linguistic. If the Indo-European Greek gloried in his
sculpture and architecture and the Hebrew in his Psalm, the Arabian
gloried in his ode (*qasidah*).

Medieval Arabs continued in that tradition. "The beauty of a
woman," declares an adage of theirs, "lies in her face; the beauty of
man in the eloquence of his tongue." "Wisdom," according to a late
saying, "alighted on three: the brain of the Frank [Western Euro-
pean], the hand of the Chinese, and the tongue of the Arabian." Modern

audiences in such cities as Cairo, Damascus, and Baghdad can be moved to a feverish pitch by the recital of poems or the delivery of orations in classical Arabic which they only vaguely comprehend. Something in the rhythm, the rhyme, and the music exercises on them what amounts to hypnotic effect. They have a term for it: "legitimate magic" (*sihr halal*).

I

ISLAM made full use of this linguistic phenomenon and psychological peculiarity. If Christianity's focus centered on a personality, Islam's was on a book.

The book is entitled *Qur'an* (Koran). Etymologically the term simply means "reading"; theologically it means the word of God incarnate. It is eternal and uncreated. The Arabic copy that a Moslem uses today is an exact replica of a heavenly prototype, dictated word by word to the Prophet Muhammad. "And lo, it is in the Mother of the Book in Our presence, exalted, wise" (43:3); "Nay, but it is a glorious Koran on a guarded tablet" (85:21–2; cf. 56:76–7).

This metaphysical concept of heavenly prototypes did not originate in Islam. It belongs to a cycle of thought that can be traced back to the dawn of history. The Sumerians, originators of the Euphratean civilization, believed that their temples on earth had counterparts in the sky. Their Semitic successors in the area picked up the idea. The Hebrews personified Wisdom, made her a goddess, and viewed her as existing by Yahweh's side from the beginning (Prov. 8:22 et seq.). Plato correlated the concept of "idea" with "being" as the permanent, self-existing, transcendent entity. It became the perfect model for the imperfect copies we see around us. Hence such expressions as "the ideal teacher," as if somewhere there existed or exists a perfect teacher of which this one is a replica. In his Revelation (21:10 et seq.) John the Divine saw a heavenly Jerusalem, which he described in detail. We still sing of this heavenly Jerusalem in our Sunday services.

In Christianity the word of God (Logos) becomes Christ (John 1:1); in Islam it becomes the Koran. This makes the Koran more than a bible of its religion. It makes it a participant in a way similar to the host in the Roman Catholic Church. "None but the purified shall touch it" (56:78). An old-fashioned Moslem goes through the legal ablution before he opens the book. He never puts it beneath another book, never reads it except in a reverential tone and posture. If he is a book dealer, he won't sell the book. He bestows a copy on the would-be purchaser, who in turn bestows a specified sum of money — an act of mutual bestowal, but not a business transaction.

The Bible, as the word indicates, is a library of books written in different languages, by different men, in different places, at different times. The period covers about eight hundred and fifty years. The Koran was produced in a few years by one man who was living in one area. The Bible is inspired; the Koran is dictated. Any quotation from the Koran can be introduced with "saith Allah." Biblical text has been subjected to editorial and emendatory treatment, but not the koranic. The Koran itself sets forth the few permissible variant readings. In its phonetic and graphic reproduction, as well as in its linguistic form, the koranic text is identical with its celestial original. No Moslem, whatever his native tongue may be, should use the Koran except in its Arabic original. No followers of Muhammad, other than the Kemalist Turks, are known to have violated that rule. A paraphrase of the text is permissible for the benefit of a non-Arab, but that is not the Koran.

Without the benefit of a computer every word in this book has been counted (77,934), every letter (323,621), and every verse (6,236). In length the Koran is no more than four-fifths that of the New Testament, but in use it far exceeds it. Not only is it the basis of the religion, the canon of ethical and moral life, but also the textbook in which the Moslem begins his study of language, science, theology, and jurisprudence. Its literary influence has been incalculable and enduring. The first prose book in Arabic, it set the style for future products. It kept the language uniform. So whereas today a Moroccan uses a dialect different from that used by an Arabian or an Iraqi, all write in the same style.

The style of the Koran is God's style. It is different — incomparable and inimitable. This is basically what constitutes the "miraculous character" (*i'jaz*) of the Koran. Of all miracles it is the greatest: if all men and jinn were to collaborate, they could not produce its like (17:90). The Prophet was authorized to challenge his critics to produce something comparable (10:39). The challenge was taken up by more than one stylist in Arabic literature — with a predictable conclusion. The relevance of Muhammad's "illiteracy" to this argument becomes obvious.

In a formal reading the Koran is chanted — reflecting the influence of the liturgical reading of the Syrian Christian Scripture. But Islamic chanting (*tajwid*) has been developed into a science and an art. With chanting, the beauty of the koranic style, the charm of its cadence, the music of its rhyme, and the sequence of its rhythm are heightened. Most if not all of that artistic merit and emotional appeal is lost by translation.

The first translation into a foreign language was into Latin (ca. 1141); it was sponsored by Peter the Venerable, abbot of Cluny (France), and intended to refute the beliefs of Islam. Another work of the abbot was entitled *The Execrable Sect of the Saracens.* For five centuries the only translation was in Latin. In 1649 the first English rendition appeared in London — *The Alcoran of Mahomet,* "translated out of Arabique into French . . . and newly Englished, for the satisfaction of all that desire to look into the Turkish vanities." Other early versions in European languages were introduced by equally condemnatory statements. The first English translation from the original (by George Sale) did not appear until 1734. Writing in 1840, Thomas Carlyle, whose choice of Muhammad as the hero-prophet indicates special respect, described his holy book as "a wearisome confused jumble, crude, incondite." In truth the Koran is a literary monument of a culture and should be studied in the light of the religious, political, social, and economic aspects of that culture.

II

AS A legislator Muhammad treated specific situations as they arose, with the result that the legislative material is spread amidst other prophetic utterances and in many places out of context. In addition to rules governing prayer, fasting, pilgrimage, and other religious practices, there are ordinances relating to marriage and divorce, usury and slavery, food and drink, war prisoners and booty. The legislation is totalitarian in the sense that it covers the entire spectrum of human activity. The richest in such material is surah 2, the earliest Medinese surah and the longest in the entire book (287 verses).

28

Polygamy is a feature closely associated with Islam in the Western mind. The authorizing passage is one of the most controversial in the entire text: "Marry such women as seem good to you, two, three or four; but if ye fear that ye will not be equitable, then only one, or what your right hands own [slaves]" (4:3; cf. 70:29–30). The prescription is usually taken to mean no man should marry more than four wives. It then limits rather than introduces the plurality of spouses. It may, however, be taken as encouraging men with only one wife to marry as many as three other wives. Certain modern reformers put an entirely different interpretation on the passage, arguing that since absolute justice cannot be maintained by a husband with four wives, the intent of the injunction is monogamous. This seems farfetched. If the situation is humanly impossible why legislate for it?

The Koran like the Old Testament takes slavery for granted. So deeply rooted was the institution in the socioeconomic life of the ancient society that no other course could have been possible. Not only did Muhammad dam a main source of slavery by prohibiting inter-Moslem raiding and warring, but he introduced more humane treatment for slaves. "Be kind unto parents . . . and unto those whom your right hands own" (4:40; 16:73; 24:33). No Moslem could enslave a fellow Moslem. If a slave ('abd) embraced Islam he was not automatically freed, but manumission of slaves in general was inculcated as something pleasing to Allah; it could be regarded as an expiation for sins committed. It is generally believed that on the whole slaves fared better under Islam than in Christendom. In fact one could go further and claim that Islam has achieved a larger measure of success in dealing with the racial problem than Christianity.

Another distinctive feature of koranic legislation is the triple prohibition of usury, gambling, and wine. The tenor of the pertinent passages and the context in which they occur suggest that the legislation was prompted by immediate local situations. The ordinance against usury (riba, 2:276–8; 3:125; 4:157–9; 5:67–9) was evidently directed against Medinese Jews at a time when Muhammad sorely needed financial support while they insisted on charging interest. Gambling and wine are associated in the prohibiting injunctions, and at least gambling seems to have had some heathen connection. A favorite form of gambling involved a lottery using arrows or divining rods kept in the Kaabah (5:92). The Prophet's attitude toward wine evolved from approval (16:69) to compromise (2:216) to hostility (4:46). The passage "draw not near to prayer when ye are drunken" provides the immediate occasion for the interdiction.

III

THE purely religious legislative material in the Koran is equally haphazard and disjointed. Muhammad, in common with Christ, was neither a theologian nor one who set out with a ready-made system of beliefs and practices. His revelations had to wait a couple of hundred years before they were systematized by theologians. The Nicene Creed was not formulated until three hundred years after Christ's death. The nearest to an outline of the Moslem creed occurs in surah 4 verse 135:

> O believers, believe in Allah and His Messenger
> and the Book He hath sent down unto His Messenger
> and the Book He sent down before.
> Whoso disbelieveth in Allah and His angels and His
> Books and His messengers and the last day hath
> surely gone astray into far error.

In dealing with the fundamentals of their religion, Moslem theologians distinguish between "beliefs" (*iman*, "rendering secure [through surrender]") and "duties" or "acts of worship" (*'ibadat*). The beliefs are summed up in six dogmas relating to God, Muhammad, the Koran, the angels, sin, and the last day. The concept of God permeates the entire system of Islamic theology. The system emphasizes his essence, his attributes, and his works. He is one, unique, the supreme reality, eternal, preexistent, and self-subsistent (112:2; 2:256; 3:1). He has ninety-nine attributes, which become his excellent names (7:179). God is the Omniscient, the Omnipresent (13:9 et seq.; 6:59 et seq.; 3:25–7), the Omnipotent, and so on. His attributes of might and majesty, however, overshadow those of love. He thereby partakes more of the nature of the Old Testament deity than of the New Testament one:

> He is Allah, there is no god but He.
> He is the knower of the invisible and the visible;
> He is the merciful, the compassionate.

30

He is Allah, there is no god but He.
He is the sovereign, the holy, the peaceable,
  the keeper of faith, the preserver,
  the mighty, the compeller, the sublime.
Glorified be Allah, above all they associate with Him.

(59:21–2)

God's works include creation, preservation, revelation, and judgment (16:3 et seq.; 2:27–8).

The second dogma in the faith treats Muhammad as God's messenger and prophet. These two dogmas of God's oneness and Muhammad's messengership constitute the confession of faith (*shahadah*). The two formulas *la ilaha illa Allah* and *Muhammadun rasulu Allah* ("there is no God whatever but Allah," "Muhammad is the messenger of Allah") do not occur jointly in the Koran. They are repeated in the daily muezzin's call to prayer and on innumerable other occasions.

The third dogma relates to the Koran as the word of God, which was discussed above. This dogma ranks high in importance and there is a wide gap between it and subsequent dogmas.

Islam arranges its angels in a hierarchy reflecting the Judeo-Christian tradition. Gabriel, as the bearer of the revelation, stands first although the Koran mentions him only once in that capacity (2:91). He is, moreover, identified with the spirit of holiness (2:81; 16:104) and the faithful spirit (26:193). Other angels have different functions as guardians, writers, recorders (82:10–2), and messengers (35:1). Created of light, angels are resplendent, sexless, and immortal.

The idea of the devil as a fallen angel likewise stems from the earlier Semitic tradition. The Hebrew origin of the name Shaytan (Satan, "adversary") confirms it. Shaytan is the enemy of God, the chief of evil spirits who specializes in leading men astray. He is, in the theologians' opinion, ugly, made of fire, and may be male or female. He can appear in human form without betraying his identity. Another name of his is Iblis (Gr. Diabolus). Iblis was the one who, when God created Adam and ordered the angels to bow down before him, refused (2:32 et seq.; 7:10 et seq.). He was then cursed and banished and has since made it his business to induce men to disobey God.

Sin has two varieties, ceremonial and ethical. The only unpardonable sin is associating with the one God other deities (*shirk*, 4:51,

116). Moslems pride themselves on being the only unitarians. Ascribing plurality to the deity contravenes the basic dogma of Islam. Hence the reiterated condemnation of polytheists and threat of their final judgment. Strictly, Christians and Jews, the "people of the book," were not considered polytheists, but some commentators on the following verse have taken a different view: "Lo! the unbelievers of the 'people of the book' and the idolaters shall abide in the fire of Hell. They are the worst of all creatures" (98:5).

Of all verses in the Koran those dealing with the sixth dogma — the final judgment and life thereafter — are the most impressive. Eschatology figured prominently in Muhammad's mind. Like Christ he at times must have felt that the final day was imminent, but he made more use of it as a motif in his preaching. He refers to it in various forms, such as "the day of judgment" (15:35–6; 82:17–8), "the day of resurrection" (22:5; 30:56), "the day" (24:24–5; 31:32), "the hour" (15:85; 18:20), "the indubitable" (69:1–2) and "the inevitable" (56:1). One surah (75) is dedicated to the resurrection. Both bodily pains and physical pleasures are depicted with a brush dipped in vivid colors. Next to polygamy this emphasis on the physical is the feature that distinguishes Islam in Western Christian eyes.

> Those on the right hand, what are those on the right hand? . . .
> Those are they who are brought nigh
> in gardens of delight. . . .
> On couches inlaid [with jewels]
> they shall recline facing one another,
> while wait on them immortal youths
> with goblets and ewers and a cup from pure spring,
> therefrom they suffer no aching of the head nor any madness,
> and such fruit as they may choose
> and such flesh of fowl as they may desire.
> And there are large-eyed lovely damsels [sing. *huri*, houri]
> like unto hidden pearls,
> a reward for what they used to do. . . .
>
> And those on the left hand; what are those on the left hand?
> They are amid scorching wind [*samum*, simoom] and scalding
> water
> and shadow of black smoke,
> neither cool nor refreshing.
>
> (56:8–23; 40–3)

Beliefs are not enough. They should be supplemented with acts of worship referred to as the five pillars of faith. Prescribed in the Koran, these religious duties are incumbent on all believers, male and female.

First among the pillars is the profession of faith (*shahadah*) summed up in the musical formula *la ilaha illa Allah; Muhammadun rasulu Allah*. To believe at heart in the oneness of God and the messengership of Muhammad does not suffice: one should declare openly his belief. The mere pronouncement of the formula is an act of piety. The formula is therefore almost constantly on believers' lips. Such is the importance of this profession that if a non-Moslem accepts and reproduces it he becomes at least nominally a Moslem — but he should then proceed to the performance of the remaining duties.

Prayer stands as the pillar of faith that is next in importance. There are two kinds of prayer: the spontaneous, extemporaneous one (*du'a'*) prompted by the exigencies of the situation, and the formal, institutional one (*salah*) for which ceremonial cleanliness, involving ablution, is a prerequisite (2:239; 24:57). This ritual prayer is legally prescribed at stated times and performed with specified bodily gestures and genuflections and with orientation toward Mecca. Stereotyped phrases are recited in Arabic. This prayer is synchronized with the muezzin's call to prayer five times a day. Its object is not so much petitioning Allah for favors as it is glorifying him and acknowledging his oneness, his might and majesty. The bodily movements, culminating in prostrating oneself to the point of touching the ground with the forehead, befit the words uttered in adoration. "Mosque" is a corruption of *masjid*, meaning "place of prostration."

The pre-Islamic form of prayer must have been generally unorganized and informal. The elaborate Moslem system displays, in its orientation and bodily movements, Christian influence. That *salah* is a loanword from Aramaic is indicated by its orthography (with a *waw* rather than an *alif*). The evolution of the institution of prayer in Muhammad's mind is noticeable: in general it is encouraged in a Meccan revelation (87:15), but its requirements are set forth in later Medinese surahs (2:239; 4:57; 11:116; 30:16–7; 50:38–9). Even then, only three prayers seem to be specified. The night prayer, which has for an antecedent a Syrian Christian monks' practice, is voluntary but meritorious as a work of supererogation (17:81; 50:38–9). The number five (at dawn, noon, mid-afternoon, sunset, and early evening) for the daily obligatory prayers was arrived at on the occasion of Muhammad's miraculous ascent to heaven, according to al-Bukhari whose collection of traditions (sing. *hadith*, "a saying ascribed to the Prophet") is considered sound and genuine. Allah first asked for fifty times of daily prayer, but Muhammad was advised by Abraham to go back more than once and bargain for a smaller number. The story is reminiscent of Abraham's bargaining with God on behalf of Sodom and Gomorrah (Gen. 18:23 et seq.).

Only one congregational prayer is enjoined, the one on Friday at noon (62:9). Friday may be considered a counterpart of the Jewish Sabbath and the Christian Sunday although it is not a day of rest. The noon service features an address — short, incisive, and rich in koranic quotations — which is sometimes flavored with political exhortations. Some of the most violent uprisings against the French mandate in Syria followed Friday noon sermons at the Umayyad Mosque in Damascus. Women's attendance is not obligatory. The occasion of congregational prayer has proved useful for military drill in that worshipers are required to stand throughout the service in rows, with spaces in between for prostration, and to chant the ritual in unison.

The story of Muhammad's celestial ascent (*mi'raj*) is based on a solitary, vague verse: "Glorified be He who made His servant journey by night from the Holy Mosque to the farther mosque [*al-aqsa*], the neighborhood whereof We have blessed" (17:1). The dramatic ascent was preceded by an equally dramatic episode involving instant transportation on a curious mount from Mecca to Jerusalem (*isra'*). If Moses spoke to God face to face on Mt. Sinai, if Enoch before him walked with God, and if Jesus established a sonship with Him, why could not Muhammad do something similar? A critical modern scholar, however, spoils the drama. The nocturnal journey, he argues, was not to Jerusalem but to a settlement near Mecca where there was a mosque named al-Aqsa.

Embellished by later accretions echoing Christian traditions, the trip became the center of a cycle of elaborate stories especially favored in mystic circles. It is now believed that it served as a prototype for

Dante's *Divine Comedy*. The story of the ascent added to the sanctity of Jerusalem, making it the third most important city after Mecca and Medina. The designation of Jerusalem as the Moslem rendezvous on the day of judgment added another dimension to its importance. Some of the most serious Israeli-Arab outbreaks under the British mandate and later centered on the Jewish Wailing Wall, associated by Moslems with the halting place of the Prophet's mount. The ascension is commemorated annually throughout the night of the twenty-eighth of Rajab, when mosques are lit up and special services are held.

As in the case of prayer, almsgiving — the third pillar — falls into two categories: voluntary, practiced as an act of love and piety (2: 263–9, 273–5, called *sadaqah*), and obligatory or legal (2:40, 77; 9:5, styled *zakah*). Zakah and salah are often mentioned in the same koranic verses, giving zakah a high rank. Indeed zakah is one of the prominent features of the religion. It is stressed not only as a social obligation but also as a means of self-purification. The Arabic orthography of this word, as in the case of salah, suggests a Semitic origin. Zakah's underlying principle tallies with the tithe which South Arabian merchants paid to the local deity before they could sell their goods. The exact amount of zakah varied but was later fixed by canon law at 2½ percent of the individual's income. It may be paid in money or in cattle, corn, fruit, merchandise, or other products. Sadaqah was a free-will act of charity not limited to Moslems, but zakah was a purely denominational institution involving alms raised from Moslems and distributed among Moslems. Even soldiers' pensions were not exempt.

In the early days of the Islamic state officials collected zakah and held it in a central treasury. It was used to support the needy in the community as well as for building mosques and defraying government expenses (9:60). With the disintegration of the purely Islamic state, zakah was left to the believer's conscience to be replaced in later times by Western-modeled taxation. Nevertheless it is still practiced as a meritorious act.

Fasting, the fourth act of worship, is another ancient Judeo-Christian institution. Christ fasted forty days and nights (Matt. 4:2); so did Moses (Deut. 9:4) and after him Elijah (1 Kings 19:8). All three observed fasting in preparation for some supernatural experience. Baby-

35

lonians and Egyptians practiced abstinence from food for different purposes. Arabians in pre-Islam had periods of penance (*tahannuth*), but whether that penance included abstinence from food is not certain. The Islamic revelation prescribing fasting "as it was prescribed to those preceding you" (2:179) acknowledges the relation to an earlier monotheistic practice.

The evolution of the idea of instituting fasting as a fundamental pillar of faith is interesting to observe. There is no evidence that while in Mecca the Prophet ever fasted. As a matter of fact the word for fasting (*sawm*) occurs in only one Meccan surah (19:27), where the context suggests abstaining from talking. In his early Medinese period the Prophet evidently observed the tenth of Muharram (*'ashura'*) as a day of fasting, clearly an adaptation of a Jewish practice (Lev. 16:29). In this period several references to fasting occur (2:192; 4:94; 19:27; 58:5) prescribing it as a penitential or an expiratory measure, with no specification as to the kind or duration of the abstinence. Finally Ramadan was fixed in one single passage:

> . . . the month of Ramadan, wherein the Koran
> was sent down as a guidance to all men
> and as evidences of the guidance
> and as a criterion of right and wrong.
> So whoever of you is then at home
> let him fast the month.
> And whoever of you is sick or on a journey
> let him fast the same number of other days.
>
> (2:181)

Ramadan, besides being the revelation month, was a holy one before Islam and the victory of Badr. It is the ninth month of the lunar year and progressively moves through all seasons of the solar year. Since food and drink (as well as sexual relations) are forbidden from the time "a white thread can be distinguished from a black thread" till sunset, fasting becomes particularly trying when it occurs in summer. Those who can afford it convert day into night by staying awake and eating all night, and sleeping all day. The beginning of the month is marked by the appearance of the new moon. Customarily sunrise is proclaimed by an early-morning crier who, beating a drum, goes around awakening the faithful. Sunset is marked by the firing of a cannon.

Modern Moslems make more display of fasting than of individual prayer. Western-educated young men who are hardly ever seen in the act of prayer insist when in public places on having breakfasts served before dawn and suppers after sunset. Abstinence, primarily an act of self-denial, when used for expiation commands a high value. A hadith in al-Bukhari promises forgiveness of all past sins to him who keeps Ramadan in faith and for Allah's sake.

Pilgrimage (*hajj*) is another institution which lends itself to public display, and it is the fifth pillar of faith. Journeying to visit sacred places and engage in religious ceremonies antedates monotheism, as is evidenced by echoes of the practice which resound in the Old Testament. Early Hebrews were repeatedly commanded to go three times a year "before the Lord God" (Exod. 23:14, 17; 34:22). The early-Christian urge "to tread the path trodden by the Savior" received special impetus when Helena, mother of Constantine the Great, visited Jerusalem about 325, discovered the "true cross," and founded the Church of the Holy Sepulcher and the Church of Nativity. The Crusades were fought partially to ensure the safety of visitors to the Holy Land. There is reason to believe pilgrimage in Arabia originated at the autumnal equinox to bid farewell to the harsh rule of the summer sun and to welcome the advent of the god of thunder (Quzah; "rainbow" in Ar. is "Quzah's bow"), who ushers in a period of humidity and fertility. With the religious ceremonies were associated fairs that added economic and social importance to the annual occasions.

Young Muhammad no doubt participated in such ceremonies, but not after his call. Nowhere in the Meccan surahs can any trace of the hajj be detected. Beginning with the second year of the hijrah the Prophet began to bring the Kaabah, the focus of the pilgrimage, toward the center of his system. Abraham, father of monotheism, was named as the Kaabah's founder (2:119; 3:91; 22:27–30). It soon replaced Jerusalem as the qiblah for prayer (2:138–40). Finally the divine command crystallized, making the Kaabah the object of the major pilgrimage (to be undertaken collectively at a stated time) and of the minor pilgrimage (*'umrah*) (whose timing is left to the convenience of the individual).

Fulfill the major and the minor pilgrimages unto Allah;
but if ye are prevented
then make such offering [animal for sacrifice] as
    may be feasible,
and shave not your heads
till the offering reaches its destination.
If any of you is sick or suffering from a head injury,
then a compensation by fasting, almsgiving or other
    pious observance.

(2:192)

In addition to letting his hair grow while in a state of sanctity (*ihram*), the pilgrim is required to wear a white seamless garment and to abstain from sexual relations, shedding blood, hunting, and uprooting plants (5:1–2, 96; 22:27–37). The first two weeks of dhu-al-Hijjah, the month to which the pilgrimage gives its name, were designated for the major pilgrimage. Muhammad had no chance to undertake it until the fall of Mecca in the tenth year of the hijrah.

The pilgrimage rites begin with a two-day march in the course of which a halt is made and the devil is stoned. This is followed by a sevenfold circumambulation of the Kaabah and a sevenfold course between two mounds adjacent to the Kaabah. The course commemorates Hagar's run back and forth in that place in search of water. The ceremonies end with the sacrifice of a sheep or other horned domestic animal (22:36–8). This is timed on the tenth of dhu-al-Hijjah and is celebrated throughout the Moslem world as 'Id al-Adha ("the festival of sacrifice").

The well which Gabriel opened for Hagar and her son Isma'il when they were dying of thirst in the desert became known by the name of Zamzam. It lies opposite the Kaabah's southeast corner, wherein the Black Stone is lodged. Pilgrims kiss the Black Stone, drink the sacred water of the Zamzam for its health-giving property, and carry bottles of water home for healing purposes. The Black Stone was a pre-Islamic fetish. Geologists tell us it is of meteoric origin and Moslems agree: it is of heavenly origin received by Isma'il (Ishmael) while rebuilding the sanctuary with his father. At that time the instructions in the rites of the pilgrimage were revealed. Neither the Black Stone nor the Zamzam is mentioned in the Koran.

By adopting and Islamizing these ancient pagan rites, Islam kept

38

its largest heritage from pre-Islamic Arabia. The new rites distinguished the new monotheism from its two older sisters and to that extent alienated it from them.

Once a year at the proper time, Mecca becomes so religiously magnetized that it attracts hordes of men and women from the four quarters of the globe. From north and south, east and west, they converge on the city by caravan, airplane, or ship. Before the puritanical Wahhabi 'Abd-al-'Aziz ibn-Su'ud (Saud) abolished the innovative practice, Egypt, Syria, Iraq, and Yaman each sent at the head of its caravan a sumptuously decorated litter on a camel. At present the total number of participants in the annual pilgrimage is a million, of whom a quarter come from outside the Arabian peninsula. The social, economic, and intellectual effects of such gatherings are not easy to exaggerate. Next to the universal canon law (shari'ah, to be studied later) and the liturgical common use of Arabic, al-hajj ranks as the greatest unifying force in Islam. As believers — black and white, rich and poor, high and low, Arabs, Turks, Persians, Hindus, and Sudanese — worship together they heighten their awareness of the solidarity of Islam as a religious fraternity.

Before the exploitation of oil in the 1940s, pilgrimage was the greatest source of income to Arabia. It richly contributed to the improvement of communication and transportation facilities and to the development of more sanitary conditions. The gathering and the mood it engendered provided unique opportunity for the religio-political propagandist.

IV

A CHRISTIAN reviewing critically the above account of Islamic beliefs and practices would not find much that is in conflict with his own religion beyond the messengership of Muhammad and the miraculous character of the Koran. Even then he may concede that Muhammad was a messenger and the Koran was inspired to the extent that both served God's purposes. Likewise a Moslem viewing the Apostles' Creed with critical eyes would accept it with certain revisions. What he denies is more than what he affirms, but what he affirms is generally fundamental. His revised version would read as follows (the dots indicate the number of words omitted):

> I believe in God . . Almighty,
> Maker of heaven and earth;
> and in Jesus Christ . . . . .
> who was conceived by the Holy Ghost, born of the
> Virgin Mary, ...
> dead . . . . He ascended into heaven,
>
> .   .   .   .
>
> from thence He shall come . . . .
> I believe in the Holy Ghost, ...
> the forgiveness of sins,
> the Resurrection of the body, and the life
> everlasting.[1]

Thus, the reason for the alienation between the two monotheistic sisters clearly is not entirely ideological. It is historical, involving a political and military struggle for power and economic rivalry. Islam's expansion in the seventh century was largely at the expense of the Christian Byzantine Empire. For centuries after that, Saljuq and Ottoman Moslems posed a threat to the front of Europe through the Balkans, while Arabs threatened its back through Spain and its belly through Sicily and Italy. The Crusades reinforced the tradition of hostility and hatred and the mandates wrote the last chapter in its history.

[1] Cf. Alfred Guillaume, *Islam* (London, 1963), p. 194.

JURISPRUDENCE AND THEOLOGY

❖ OF ALL ancient peoples the Semites were not only the most religiously oriented but also the most legalistically minded. The Babylonian society, unlike its Sumerian predecessor, was based on divine law. Its great legislator Hammurabi (d. ca. 1686) incorporated Sumerian ordinances in his code but represented himself as receiving it directly from the sun god Shamash. The Hebrews continued the tradition. All legislation in Exodus, Leviticus, Numbers, and Deuteronomy was a direct revelation from Jehovah through Moses (Exod. 25:1, 35: 1; Deut. 6:1). The Decalogue was written by Jehovah's own hand on tablets and handed down to Moses (Exod. 24:12; 31:18). This divine origin of the Old Testament legislation constitutes one of its distinctive features.

Greek law, on the other hand, was entirely man-made; it had no religious aspect. The Greeks seem at times to have held human intellect in higher esteem than their deities. Roman law, the most highly developed of antiquity, had a divine element but was mostly of human origin. Modern law is the creation of the state. The state amends it and enforces it, with no divine interference.

I

ISLAMIC law followed the Jewish precedent. It thereby differed from Christianity, whose founder concerned himself more with things spiritual than legal. Paul, founder of Gentile Christianity, was equally spiritually minded. In the Moslem mind religious law, secular law, and theology were inextricably mixed. Religious law (*shari'ah*, literally "a watering place") was an integral part of the word of Allah incarnate. It coexisted with him. The shari'ah, according to the traditional view, is eternal, universal, perfect, fit for all men at all times in all places. It preceded the state and the society. It recognizes no difference between the sacred and the secular. It sets forth and regulates man's relations with and obligations to God as well as his relations with his fellow man. All Allah's commandments — about ritual, civil, and other matters — with their punishments are recorded in the Koran. Of the roughly six thousand verses therein, some two thousand are strictly legislative. They are mostly embraced in surahs 2 and 4.

Throughout his lifetime Muhammad served as God's spokesman, thereby performing the triple function of legislator, judge, and executive. But with his death the door through which divine legislation was received was forever closed. No prophet was to come after him. Meantime Muhammad's politico-religious community (*ummah*) was no longer limited to Medina or Arabia: it had become worldwide. It was confronted with myriad legal problems which never occurred to the revelation. New sources of legislation had to be found, and if they could not be found, they had to be created.

The usage of the Prophet (*sunnah*, "custom," "use") including his deeds, utterances, and tacit approval was available. It clarified the scriptural text, elaborated on it, supplemented it, and thus fulfilled new demands. The Prophetic sunnah became in the first century after the hijrah the object of intensive study, next to the study of the Koran itself. The research involved collection, verification, and recording. The record of an action or a saying of the Prophet became technically known as *hadith*. Hadith worked its way into second place after the Holy Book as a source of law. In the Koran the words were revealed. In the Prophetic hadith the meaning was only inspired. It was the first in a series of devices to soften the rigidity and immutability of the divine law.

In the first two centuries after Muhammad's death the number of hadiths increased in direct proportion to the demand. Whenever the community faced a new issue each party concerned would seek authority for its view in a hadith. The recurring struggle for the caliphal seat provided the greatest opportunity for the fabrication and dissemination of hadiths. This became a flourishing industry. It necessitated the development of a science unique to Islam, the science (*'ilm*) of hadith, designed to distinguish between sound and false, between probable and possible forms of tradition. Meantime the basis was widened to include utterances and practices ascribed to the Companions. Hadith in its Prophetic form was of course more authoritative than in its apostolic form.

In Medina, home of the Companions and cradle of tradition, an early school of law flourished. Its emphasis was on tradition. Its eponymous founder, Malik ibn-Anas (718–96), was a theologian-jurist who became the center of a circle of disciples that developed and transmitted his views. His lectures and the hadiths treated therein were embodied in a book (*al-Muwatta'*, "the trodden path"), the first law manual. It is still used as a text. The Maliki was the first of four orthodox schools of Islamic jurisprudence.

Meanwhile another device was contrived to broaden the base and reduce the rigidity of the divine law: personal judgment (*ra'i*, "opinion"). This judicial speculation proved a richer source than hadith. Its exponent was a Kufan grandson of a Persian slave who was neither a professional lawyer nor a judge but a businessman. Like his counterpart in Medina, abu-Hanifah (699–767) found himself the center of a circle of disciples. He wrote no books but his teachings became known through one of his pupils, a judge in the court of Harun al-Rashid. By leaning more on juridical opinion and less on tradition the Hanafi school instituted new methods of legal reasoning involving analogy (*qiyas*). Its connection with the 'Abbasid court gave it prestige and the opportunity to spread eastward. Saljuq and Ottoman Turks inherited the system and ultimately passed it on to their successor Arab states from Iraq to Egypt (but the Maliki school was favored in North Africa and Spain). The Hanafi established itself as the second orthodox school in Islam.

Between the "people of hadith" (as the Maliki school was dubbed) and the "people of opinion" (as the school of Medina was styled) there was room for a third school. It was soon filled by the Shafi'i school, so named after Muhammad ibn-Idris al-Shafi'i. Al-Shafi'i was born in Ghazzah (Gaza, 768), educated in Medina and Baghdad, and labored in Mecca, Baghdad, and Cairo, where he died in 820. He started as an eclectic reconciler of the two earlier systems of law and ended as the originator of a third orthodox system. More than that, he became the founder of the classical science of Islamic law (*fiqh*, "intelligence," as distinguished from *'ilm*, "knowledge"). His formulation of the principles of canon law became the accepted one.

Fiqh may be considered a purely Islamic science. Unlike such other sciences as mathematics, medicine, and philosophy, it had an entirely indigenous origin. In its development it was not appreciably influenced by Indo-Iranian or Indo-European thought. The founder took no interest in Roman law or Greek philosophy, though he used logical reasoning — reflecting Aristotelian logic — in his didactic and polemic works.

Al-Shafi'i's scholarly career fitted him admirably for the great task awaiting him. As professor of theology first in Mecca, the religious capital of Islam, and later in Baghdad, its intellectual capital, he had the opportunity to establish close contacts with some of the best minds of his time. His students spread his influence — and with it his reputation — far and wide. He was soon acclaimed "imam" ("religious leader"), a title reserved for the few most distinguished men. While in Baghdad, he issued the first edition of his *al-Risalah* ("the epistle"), considered the first scientific treatment of Islamic law and still a recognized textbook. In 815 the imam moved to Cairo to teach at its oldest mosque and write more works. There he was declared the "renovator of the faith" promised in a Prophetic hadith at the "head" of each century. This was the third Moslem century. Five years later he died and was buried at the foot of al-Muqattam, where his shrine still receives pilgrims and letters from all over the land seeking his intercession as a holy man.

After al-Shafi'i, fiqh came to mean the science that regulates man's relations not only with himself and his fellow men (*mu'amalat*) but also with his God (*'ibadat*). Theology becomes then a branch of jurisprudence with the jurist preceding the theologian. Fiqh provides regulations for prayer, almsgiving, fasting, pilgrimage, and other religious obligations as well as for civil, criminal, commercial, and military cases. All acts of man then fall into two comprehensive categories: what is legally permitted (*halal*) and what is legally prohibited (*haram*). The permitted has several gradations ranging from "obligatory" to "desirable" to "indifferent."

Al-Shafi'i's starting point was the already established view that the ultimate source of legislation was the Book of Allah and that all other sources were subsidiary to it. He then added a reservation: subsidiary sources should stem from the Koran. To be accepted a law should be implicitly, if not explicitly, derived from the Word of Allah. The Prophetic sunnah, which he defined as the Prophet's model behavior, was fully acceptable. More than once the Koran commands the Moslem to believe in Allah and in his Messenger (7:158; 64:8; cf. 4:169; 59:7), but there was no justification for accepting as authoritative the practices or sayings of the Companions or their successors. Not only did al-Shafi'i thereby limit the sunnah to that of the Prophet, but he insisted on its verification and authentication. To be valid a hadith should consist of two parts: a chain of authorities (*isnad*) and a text (*matn*). The chain of authorities transmitting the hadith should go back to the Prophet uninterruptedly. Authenticated hadiths should agree. If they do not, the one more in keeping with the Koran is the one acceptable. A Prophetic hadith when thus established acquires an authority approaching that of a koranic text, the only difference being that in the Koran Allah speaks, in a hadith the Prophet speaks.

Before al-Shafi'i's time jurists had discovered a new source of legislation — consensus (*ijma'*, "agreement") — and raised it to the third rank after the Koran and the hadith. But there was no agreement among them on what constituted ijma'. Al-Shafi'i accepted ijma' as a source and defined it as "the public opinion of the Moslem community as expressed through its most learned jurists." It was more a de facto agreement than one arrived at formally at a council. It was not easy, however, to find sanction for this doctrine in the Koran. The reference to the believers as a "middle community" (2:137) is rather farfetched. After al-Shafi'i, tradition generously offered the desired justification. A Prophetic hadith was "discovered": "My community shall not agree on an error."

The door of revelation was closed with the Prophet's death; that of hadith was closed some three centuries later. But the door of ijma' was open forever. A present or a future community could use it for introducing radical changes in its corpus of beliefs and practices. Besides, the door of ijma' was opened so wide that it could admit practices and institutions of pre-Islamic origin. Circumcision, an early Semitic custom, thus became a hallmark of Islam corresponding to baptism in Christianity. The sinlessness of the Prophet and his miracle-working ability were admitted into folk belief. So was the cult of saints. Through ijma' the basis of sunnah came to mean the theory and practice of the catholic Moslem community.

But the Shi'ah, the dissident sect and a large minority, had no use for ijma'. Its adherents substituted for it an infallible imam (*mahdi*, "[divinely] guided"), a descendant of the Prophet through his daughter Fatimah and her husband 'Ali. They endowed their imam with the sole right of determining what believers should and should not do. Nor did the Shi'ah accept the Sunnite hadiths. They had their own corpus of law with their own jurists and theologians.

Analogy (*qiyas*, "measurements") was the fourth and last source of canon law. This was a form of the legal opinion recognized earlier — a variation of the Hanafi school. It involved first establishing a parallel between a case treated in the Koran or by the Prophet and one newly arisen, and then proceeding to a logical deduction. This procedure was even more difficult than the others to justify on koranic basis. Al-Shafi'i accepted it hesitatingly and with reservations. Qiyas should be limited to cases untreated in the Koran or by the Prophet, and the consideration should go beyond the points of resemblance to the reason (*'illah*) behind the ruling.

Adherents of the fourth and last orthodox school of Islamic law, the Hanbali, categorically rejected ijma' and reserved qiyas for rare cases of sheer necessity. The founder Ahmad ibn-Hanbal (d. 855) studied at Baghdad under al-Shafi'i, whom he admired but with whom he later disagreed. Ibn-Hanbal concentrated on the Koran and tradition. His school became the most conservative and literalist of all four. His unswerving allegiance to tradition earned him disciples and admirers and subjected him to imprisonment and severe punishment under the unorthodox caliph al-Ma'mun. Today the most notable adherents of his system are the Wahhabis of Su'udi Arabia.

Every Sunnite Moslem is supposed to belong to one of these four schools. He is at liberty to transfer his allegiance from one to the other, but so long as he owes allegiance to one its decisions are binding on him.

II

ISLAMIC law and theology started simultaneously from the same double base, Koran and tradition, and kept company for a time. Side by side with the elaboration of a system of canon law went the elaboration of a system of orthodox theology. But the theological formulation turned out to be more laborious and more complicated, requiring several generations of original thinkers and commentators. Next to the formulation of law, building a structured theology became the earliest intellectual activity in Islam and its most highly developed expression.

So long as the Moslem community was limited to isolated and insulated Arabia, it remained primitive and unsophisticated. Its members contented themselves with a practical, unspeculative form of piety. But once that community swelled, as a result of the early conquests, to the extent that it covered a large part of the area to the north, the situation changed. The Moslem mind was for the first time exposed to foreign currents of thought led by Greek philosophy and Christian theology as expounded in Syria. There were also gnostic doctrines in Iraq, dualistic in Persia and animistic beyond. The transfer of the caliphal capital in 661 from Medina to Damascus, provincial capital of the Byzantine Empire, brought Islamic and philosophic Christian thought to a point of direct confrontation.

In the early Umayyad court of Damascus, founded by Mu'awiyah (661–80), debates were held on the relative merits of Islam and Christianity. One of the participants was Saint John of Damascus (d. 748), surnamed Chrysorrhoas ("golden-mouthed"), the most learned Eastern theologian of his day. Saint John wrote a dialogue with a "Saracen" on the divinity of Christ and the problem of free will. The book was designed as a manual for the guidance of Christian debaters with Moslem opponents. This Syrian Christian, who wrote in Greek but knew Arabic and spoke Syriac, was an early agent through which Greek philosophic and Christian theologic thought found its way into Islam.

The doctrine of free will was evidently the first to agitate the Islamic mind. It stood in sharp contrast to the harsh predestination emphatically preached in the Koran as a corollary of God's almightiness (15:21; 42:26; 43:10; 54:49).

> Say: "O Allah, owner of the sovereign power,
> Thou givest power to whom Thou willest, and withdrawest
>   power from whom Thou willest.
> Thou exaltest whom Thou willest and Thou abasest
>   whom Thou willest.
> In Thy hand is all good and over all things Thou
>   hast power.

> "Thou causest the night to pass into the day, and Thou
>   causest the day to pass into the night.
> Thou bringest forth the living from the dead, and Thou
>   bringest forth the dead from the living.
> Thou providest for whom Thou willest, without reckoning."
>   (3:25–6)

This emphasis on the absolute sovereignty of God may have disposed the believers to accept whatever authority — whether political, parental, or educational — that had its sanction from above. The Arabians' feeling of helplessness vis-à-vis the relentless sun, the ruthless sandstorms, and the monotonous desert life may early have engendered in them a sense of fatalism. The consequent nonrational, almost anti-intellectual feature of Islamic orthodoxy was first challenged by a group of thinkers who adopted the doctrine of human freedom of will and called themselves Qadarites (from *qadar*, "power"). By accepting qadar they indicated their belief in man's power over his actions. This was the first school of philosophic-theologic thought in Islam. Two of the Umayyad caliphs were reportedly favorable to Qadarite teaching, but it was not until the 'Abbasid time that the full impact of their rational thought was felt.

The Baghdad school of Qadarites went by the name Mu'tazilah. The name, tradition explains, stems from a verb (*i'tazala*) meaning "to separate from." It originated when two pupils of the leading theologian Hasan al-Basri (d. 728) left his circle in protest. The Mu'tazilah made an early appearance in the 'Abbasid period, passed through many phases, including political ones, and developed more than one wing.

The rational Mu'tazilites — the liberal wing — could not accept the orthodox dogma of the Koran as the uncreated Word of Allah. Such a doctrine, they argued, would compromise his unity. It would constitute ascribing plurality to the Godhead. The Koran is Allah's book, but it is not coeternal with him. Hence they assumed the title "the people of unity." Nor could they accept the orthodox view that whatever happens is predestined and that man's fate is fixed before his birth. Such a view, they argued, would conflict with Allah's attribute of justice. Hence the second part of their title, "people of justice." They thus posed as the champions of God's oneness, opposing the notion of his plurality, his justice, and the idea of his arbitrariness. How could, they asked, an all-just deity punish a man for what that man did not freely commit? Admittedly, Allah's power is all-embracing but what he wills is different from what he commands.

This school of theology had its heyday when the seventh 'Abbasid caliph, al-Ma'mun (813–33), espoused its cause. Al-Ma'mun's extraordinary interest in Greek philosophy predisposed him to favor the Mu'-tazilah. Not only did he proclaim the dogma of the "creation [khalq] of the Koran" and raise the Mu'tazilah to a state religion, but before his death he issued an edict that any judge in the realm who did not subscribe to the new teaching could not hold his office or be appointed to one. By way of implementation the caliph instituted an inquisitorial tribunal (mihnah) — the first of its kind in Islam — for the trial and conviction of those who denied the created character of the Koran. Ironically the movement which in the hands of thinkers represented free thought became in the hands of politicians a deadly instrument for suppressing thought. The outstanding victim of the mihnah was Ahmad ibn-Hanbal, the founder of the Hanbali school of law, whose uncompromising championship of traditional orthodoxy subjected him to physical punishment and a long period of imprisonment. A successor of al-Ma'mun turned the tables (848) on the heresy and restored the old dogma.

Although the Mu'tazilah organization weakened and finally dissolved, the school can be credited with having been the first to make human intellect challenge divine revelation and the first to introduce philosophic speculation into Islamic theology. The injection of this dose of rationalism into Moslem thought had its later effects.

III

THE man credited with having exploded Mu'tazilite theological theories and reestablishing the Sunnite creed was a Basrah-born Baghdadi scholar named 'Ali al-Ash'ari (d. 935). What gave al-Ash'ari a special advantage was the fact that he started as a pupil of a Mu'tazilite theologian and later used, in his polemics against his former masters, the same weapons of logical and philosophical argumentation which they had introduced and developed. On the positive side al-Ash'ari laid the foundation of scholastic theology (*kalam*) in Islam. He was fortunate in including in his circle a number of brilliant pupils who developed and spread his views. His system received a boost when followers of al-Shafi'i found it agreeable. The alliance between the two systems was mutually beneficial. A follower of the Ash'arite system, the illustrious al-Ghazzali (whose life will be sketched in the following chapter) added an element of continuity. Ash'arite theologians (sing. *mutakallim*) have since dominated the Islamic scene. The beliefs and practices as discussed in the first chapter of this book — including the uncreated attribute of the Koran, Allah's all-embracing omnipotence, the reality of the eschatological teachings of the Koran, and their literal interpretations — represent Ash'arite views.

Of special interest is the Ash'arite solution of the troublesome issue of the day: reconciling Allah's omnipotence with man's responsibility for his action. The solution was found in the doctrine of "acquisition" (*kasb*) derived from a passage reading: "Allah burdeneth not a soul beyond its capacity. It shall be credited with what it hath acquired and shall be debited with what it hath acquired" (2:286). What the Ash'arites seem to have meant is that although man's action, good or evil, is foreordained and willed by Allah, nevertheless man is responsible because he is left the choice to act eagerly or with reservation. Vague as this reasoning may seem it somehow satisfied the theological minds that advocated it.

50

EARLIER and more lasting than the Muʿtazilite schism was the division that arose with the Shiʿites. The name comes from a word meaning "to be a partisan of" (in this case, of ʿAli). The issue on which the Shiʿah split from the Sunnah was the headship of the community — the caliphate. Thus, in common with other schismatic sects of Islam, the Shiʿite had a political rather than a doctrinal basis.

ʿAli's partisans clung to the belief that he — the fourth of the Medinese caliphs (632–61) — was the only legitimate successor to his father-in-law Muhammad and should have been the first. He was divinely designated as imam with the authority to transmit the position to his descendants, the only descendants of the Prophet through his favorite daughter Fatimah. This is the counterpart of the divine right of kings of medieval Christendom. To the Sunnites the caliph was only a secular head of the state, with no authority to initiate or expound religious dogma. To the Shiʿites the imam was a spiritual as well as a secular ruler with authority from on high. The Sunnites made a book — the Koran — the intermediary between the worshiped and the worshiper; the Shiʿites made the intermediary between the two a person — the imam.

As a divinely designated leader, the imam was in due course endowed with immunity from error and sin. To move from there to his consideration as an incarnation of the Godhead was but a short step. A number of extremist Shiʿite followers, headed by the Ismaʿili, took this final step and alienated themselves from the body of Islam. The Ismaʿilis, or Seveners, were followers of Ismaʿil (d. 760), whom they considered the seventh and last imam after ʿAli through his son al-Husayn (d. 680). The Druzes of Lebanon and the Nusayris of Syria are offshoots from Ismaʿilism. Another offshoot added to the European vocabulary the word "assassin."

The majority of the Shiʿites, however, bypassed Ismaʿil in favor of his brother and his brother's descendants down to Muhammad al-Muntazar ("the expected," d. 878). This Muhammad was considered by them the twelfth and last imam — hence their sobriquet "Twelvers." Iran is the modern fort of the Twelvers; they also flourish in Iraq and Yaman and are represented in Lebanon and Syria.

In the course of its evolution Shi'ism absorbed a variety of ethnic and doctrinal elements supplied by malcontents and nonconformists. The bulk of those who took shelter under its umbrella were new converts to Islam from among the conquered peoples. What they resented most was Arabian ascendancy, especially under the Umayyads, and the discrepancy between the promise of equality and the achievement of it. The followers of 'Ali then came to pose a political threat to the established order whether in Damascus or Baghdad. At times they rose in open rebellion and were subjected to ruthless persecution by Umayyad and 'Abbasid caliphs. As their ranks were decimated, certain groups went underground. A number of their imams were secretly or openly killed. It was then found necessary to keep the imam in hiding pending the advent of the appropriate time for his reappearance as the mahdi. To the Seveners Isma'il became the hidden imam, and to the Twelvers, Muhammad al-Muntazar. At his reappearance the mahdi would lead his followers to ultimate victory and would fill the world with justice and peace. Clearly this was a reflection of the Judaeo-Christian Messianic idea. Psychologically it was the personification of a cherished hope among a frustrated, persecuted minority. The mahdi concept generated a rich apocalyptic literature and is still an effective power in Islam. In modern times the British had to contend with two mahdis, one in Sudan and one in Somaliland.

Other strange doctrinal principles adopted by the nonconformist Shi'ites include dissimulation and temporary marriage. For dissimulation (*taqiyah*) they found justification in such passages as "Whether ye conceal what is in your hearts or reveal it, Allah knoweth it" (3:27) and "Whoever disbelieveth in Allah after having believed — save him who is compelled and whose heart is still at peace in belief — and whoever findeth ease in belief, upon them is the wrath of Allah" (16: 108). A suppressed minority fearful of its decimation, if not extinction, the Shi'ites featured these two practices of dissimulation and temporary marriage.

Shi'ites found justification for temporary marriage (*mut'ah*, "enjoyment") in a passage (4:28) which, after listing categories of women with whom marriage is forbidden, proceeds: "And further, ye are permitted to seek out wives with your wealth in modest conduct but not in debauchery. And those of whom ye seek to enjoy [*istamta'tum*] give them their hire." Sunnite exegetes in general rejected the Shi'ite interpretation of this passage. But several of them accepted the interpretation of those passages authorizing the believer, if compelled by adverse circumstances, to profess unbelief with his tongue while affirming belief in his heart. After the Christian reconquest of the Moslem territory in Spain dissimulation was generally practiced on a large scale. Moslems adopted double names: one for use in public and the other in private. We also know of non-Moslems — Jews, for instance, in medieval Europe — who resorted to the same practice.

In addition to the Sunnite and Shi'ite forms in which Islamic piety expressed itself there was the mystic (technically, Sufi) form. The mystic approach and procedure differed radically from those of the jurist or theologian, whether Sunnite or Shi'ite. The role played by mysticism in Islam will be considered next.

SUFISM: A FEATURE OF ISLAMIC PIETY

❖ MYSTICISM as a religious phenomenon is shared not only by the three Scriptured religions but by all other great religions, including Hinduism and Taoism. Every religious tradition has a mystical aspect, involving a mystery behind the veil separating the human from the superhuman, and there have always been those with the earnest desire to penetrate that veil. These individuals or groups in all religious denominations are not satisfied with the offerings of their established systems; they yearn for personal communion with God. Such daring souls venture to plunge into an uncharted sea.

Being personal, that is, subjective and emotional, mysticism varies from one religion to another, and within the same religion from one group — or even from one individual — to another. Since it is based on individual experience it is impossible to systematize. Mysticism even defies definition. Perhaps the best attempt at a definition was made by an early fifteenth-century chancellor of the University of Paris: "Mystical theology is knowledge of God by experience arrived at through the embrace of unifying love." This sets mystical theology against dogmatic theology, which is arrived at through revelation (discussed in the preceding chapter), as well as against natural theology, which is an attempt to know God through reason and intellectual processes.

The Koran repeatedly admonishes true believers to recognize Allah through the evidence provided by nature. In an eloquent verse it proclaims:

> Verily in the creation of the heavens and the earth,
> and the alternation of night and day;
> and in the ships that move through the sea with
>   what is useful to man,
> and in the rain which Allah sendeth down from heaven,
> to give life to earth that is dead
> and to spread over it all kinds of animals;
> and in the change of winds,
> and in the clouds freely serving between heaven and earth;
> — in all these are signs for those who understand.
>
> (2:159)

I

THE word "mysticism" (from Gr. "related to mystery") has more than a religious connotation, and it lacks an Arabic correspondent. In English the word "Sufism" (from Ar. *suf*, "wool"), has only a religious connotation and is restricted in use to references to the Islamic religion. Arabic-speaking Christians never use it to describe their form of mysticism. From Arabic the term was borrowed by Turkish, Persian, Urdu, and other Islamic languages.

The word gained currency beginning about A.D. 800 when, in imitation of Christian monks, Moslem mystics began to wear coarse woolen garments. This, however, does not mean that Sufism owes its origin to Christian influence. Sufis claim as their predecessor the pious figure Hasan al-Basri of Iraq (d. 728), whose asceticism stands out in contrast to the worldly spirit which by then had pervaded all ranks of Islamic society. Earlier Moslem generations seem to have been satisfied with the two paths open to the knowledge of God: the belief in him and the practicing of his commands — the theological and the juridical paths. The dogmas and creeds worked out by theologians, as well as the rules and regulations elaborated by jurists, were uncompromisingly accepted. The general image of the deity, as revealed in the Koran and portrayed by the learned, was that of a transcendent being, infinite, arbitrary, and absolute ruler of the universe and of his impotent slaves, who "comprehend nothing of His knowledge save what He willeth" (2:256). The general atmosphere of Islam in its childhood

55

must have been fatalistic, with fear as the mainspring of its piety: fear of Allah, ruler of the day of judgment, and fear of Hell whose torments were vividly depicted in his Book. That God could reveal himself through love does not seem to have occurred to many.

Those mystically inclined believers reacted against orthodox approaches to religion and could not acquiesce in their conclusions. The wranglings of the ulama, the arguments of the canonists, and the hair-splitting discussions of the philosophers failed to satisfy them. Polemics and dialectics offered no spiritual nourishment. To them the classical theologians' God was a dead one; their search was for a personal, intimate, warm God, one who dwells not only in heaven and on earth but in the hearts of men. The system they developed was more of a philosophy than a set of doctrines.

Like members of other movements in Islam the mystics sought justification in the Word of Allah. They found it: "And if My servants question thee [the Prophet] about Me, lo, I am near" (2:182); "We are nearer to man than his jugular vein" (50:15); "And whithersoever ye turn, there is Allah's countenance" (2:109). As always, tradition was ready to lend its support. Said Muhammad: "Worship as if thou seest Him; and if thou seest Him not, yet He seest thee."

The mystic — whether he is a follower of Moses, Christ, or Muhammad — describes his spiritual experience in terms of a journey. The ultimate goal for all three is identical: union with the divine.

Arduous and long is the path (*tariqah*) of the Sufi. A lone traveler, he goes through many stages and experiences varied states. The first stage is asceticism. Asceticism involves penitence as a means of purification, renunciation of worldly affairs, and mortification. Abstaining from lawful pleasures is the first step. Not only should the novice deprive himself of property, but he should rid himself of any desire for it. He thereby acquires merits with God. With asceticism go contemplation and quietism. By weaning the soul from those pleasures to which it is accustomed the practitioner develops the quality of self-discipline, a prerequisite of mortification. By losing his self, the ascetic finds it in the universal self.

Voluntary poverty, ascetics assert, encourages dependence on God

56

and trust in him (*tawakkul*). Total trust in God sustains man in his trying experience and replaces his fear with hope. "And when," enjoins the Koran (3:153), "thou makest up thy mind, put thy trust in Allah; verily Allah loveth those who trust [in Him]." The formula "I trust in Allah" has through the ages been a favorite with believers. It is reiterated as one leaves his home, rides a mount, starts his work, or changes from one form of work to another. To be sure, the doctrine is subject to abuse, as is illustrated by the case of the dervishes, who prayed as if everything depended on God but did not work as if everything depended on themselves. According to an apocryphal story, a Bedouin complained to the Prophet that, relying on the trust principle, he left his camel outside the Prophet's residence, paid him a visit, and on his return found the camel missing. "Tie your camel's leg," admonished Muhammad; "then trust in Allah."

As Christians flocked to the fold of Islam they introduced new concepts from their mystical tradition to enrich or validate the newly rising Islamic tradition. Words were put into the mouth of the Prophet echoing those of Christ. Others were credited directly to Jesus, who according to no less an authority than Hasan al-Basri said: "My daily bread is hunger; my badge is fear, my garb is wool; my mount is my foot. . . . I have nothing, yet none is richer than I." Trust, the mystics believe, is a gateway leading to higher states of being.

Gnosis belongs to the second stage of asceticism. Its central doctrine is that there is a form of knowledge that cannot be received or imparted: knowledge that involves direct personal experience. This philosophical religious concept had a long history in the Near East before Islam. There were pre-Christian and Christian gnostic sects. Gnosticism was one of the elements absorbed by Neoplatonism from the Near East. The sources, therefore, from which Islam could have borrowed the idea were numerous.

Not all Sufis attain this high stage. Those who do, need a *shaykh* ("sheik") to serve as a guide. Such a shaykh usually surrounds himself in a mosque corner with a circle of eager and submissive disciples. The spiritual apprenticeship lasts three years. The students become linked to the teacher by emotional as well as intellectual bonds of reverence and obedience. They are then introduced to the ritual. Litanies and rituals used by Sufi orders (to be treated later) betray an Eastern Christian influence. At the graduating ceremony the diploma the shaykh bestows on the successful students takes the form of a "patched rag" (*khirqah*), the distinctive mark of the order. Here Sufism passes into an organizational stage. It starts with individuals and becomes an institution.

Illumination and love accompany gnosis. The three overlap; all are gifts from God. Far from being a passive deity the Sufi God is always actively engaged, bestowing his favors on his servants. The doctrine of illumination, like that of gnosis, was domiciled in the area before Islam's arrival. It was a favorite mystical theory of Neoplatonism and one of many Hellenistic elements that infiltrated Islam in its fourth century. The infiltration made of mysticism a syncretistic movement. The cardinal point in the theory is that God and the world of spirits are essentially "light." Our process of cognition is then illumination from above. A supreme Semitic deity was Shamash, the sun god, and one of the two supreme Zoroastrian deities was Ahura Mazda, the "lord of light."

Illumination implies emanation. Just as the rays of light emanate from the sun so do spiritual rays emanate from the Godhead. An entire surah in the Koran is dedicated to light:

> Allah is the light of the heavens and the earth.
> His light is like a niche wherein is a lamp; the
>   lamp is in glass.
> The glass is like a brilliant star, lit from
>   a blessed tree,
> an olive tree, neither of the East nor of the West,
>   whose oil would almost give light though fire
>   touched it not.
>
> (24:35)

The illumination doctrine found ready acceptance among varied ranks of Moslem society. Its adoption and exposition by Moslem philosophers (particularly ibn-Sina, Lat. Avicenna, d. 1037) gave it prestige. Not only did these philosophers preserve the concept of light as a symbol of emanation from the divine but they added a metaphysical element making light the fundamental reality of things. The illuministic movement gradually developed into a distinct school of Sufism.

58

The formulator of this school's theology was a Persian, al-Suhrawardi, who labored in Baghdad and Aleppo. While al-Suhrawardi did not add much to the metaphysical theory of light, he made it popular. In his *Hikmat al-Ishraq* ("the wisdom of illumination") he emphasized the point that all that live, move, or have being are but light. He even makes use of light to prove the existence of God. This was too much for the ulama. Under their pressure Salah-al-Din's (Saladin's) viceroy in Aleppo had him executed in 1191, when he was thirty-eight years old.

This was not the first violent encounter between Sufism and orthodoxy. As early as the mid-ninth century the Nubian Egyptian dhu-al-Nun ("he of the fish," the name for the prophet Jonah in the Koran, 21:87) was tried and sentenced for his Sufi belief. By this time the movement which had its origin in Basrah and Kufah had become widespread. Its adherents were charged with emphasizing meditation at the expense of open prayer while freeing themselves from the observances of canon law. The conservative caliph al-Mutawakkil summoned dhu-al-Nun to Baghdad and threw him into jail. Impressed by his prisoner's piety and eloquence, the caliph finally sent him back home with honors. Dhu-al-Nun is credited with being the one to introduce the doctrine of gnosis and one of the first to employ the imagery of wine and the cup in mysticism. To him has been ascribed the definition of mystic knowledge as "the communication which Allah makes of His spiritual light to the depths of our hearts."

Love became the most effective implement of the Sufis. Through it the veil of mystery can at last be rent asunder. Koranic passages emphasizing love (such as 3:29; 5:59) were interpreted by Sufis to support their concept of love. Of all Moslem sects and schools of thought, Sufism was the only one which worked out an "I-Thou" relationship based on love. The best way of expressing this Sufi-Allah relationship is to use the terms "lover" and "beloved." Love is a two-way process: the Sufi is simply in love with Allah; Allah loves those who love him. Indeed, human love is but a reflection of divine love. Gnosis, illumination, and love, therefore, meet at the point of establishing communion with the divine, a communion culminating in identification. The promised cycle is at last literally completed: "Verily we are Allah's, and verily unto Him do we return" (2:151). Thus could a Sufi enjoy the ecstasy of transcendence without the benefit of drugs.

In a Sufi woman, Rabi'ah al-'Adawiyah, mystic love found one of its earliest and noblest advocates. Rabi'ah was born at Basrah into a poor family and when young was stolen and sold as a slave. Noticing a radiance around her head as she prayed, her master freed her. Though of unusual beauty she lived a life of celibacy and otherworldliness. She soon became the center of a circle of disciples who sought her guidance in traveling the mystic path. Asked whether she hated Satan her reply was, "My love of Allah leaves no room for hating Satan." When in a dream the Prophet asked her whether she loved him, her reply was, "My love of Allah has so possessed me that no place is left for loving anyone else." Her refusal to accompany a friend for a walk on a spring day was explained on the ground that the contemplation of the Maker had turned her away from the contemplation of his works. Rabi'ah became the first saint in Sufi Islam. Among the prayers attributed to her is the following:

> O my Lord, if I worship Thee from fear of Hell,
> burn me in Hell,
> and if I worship Thee in hope of Paradise,
> exclude me thence,
> but if I worship Thee for Thine own sake
> then withhold not from me Thine Eternal Beauty.[1]

Beyond gnosis there is love, which leads to ecstasy, trance, intoxication with God, and finally self-annihilation (*fana'*) in the beloved divine. This new and rather strange doctrine in Islam brings to mind that of Buddhistic nirvana, by which it may have been inspired. Buddhism flourished on the eastern wing of the Arab empire and supplied Islam with numberless recruits. But fana' differs in not being the end. It is the opening of the door to self-perpetuation (*baqa'*) in the Godhead. The mystic passes away from an illusory earthly existence to eternal existence in the divine. For the time being, the mortal experiences the immortal. Thus fana' and baqa' become the obverse and reverse of the same coin.

[1] Margaret Smith, *Rabi'a the Mystic and Her Fellow-Saints in Islam* (Cambridge, 1928), p. 30.

This union with Allah is the ultimate goal of a Sufi career. It is the long-desired state above which there is no other.

II

TRANSITION from the union doctrine to other extreme ones was not difficult. The way lay open to monistic, pantheistic, and theosophic schools, all heresies punishable by death in the sight of orthodox Moslems. An especially conspicuous victim was a Persian, al-Hallaj ("the carder"), whose ecstatic experience in the unitive state carried him away to the extent that he identified himself with Allah. He considered himself, following the example of Jesus, God incarnate. This is the way he expressed it: "I am the Truth [haqq]."

> I am He whom I love, and He whom I love is I.
> We are two souls in one body.
> When Thou seest me, thou seest Him,
> and when thou seest Him, Thou seest us both.[2]

No more heinous sin could have been committed by a Moslem. As the heretic was being led in Baghdad to be crucified (922), he was heard praying: "As for these Thy servants, gathered to slay me in their zeal for Thy religion and in their desire to win Thy favor, forgive them, O Lord, and be Thou merciful unto them."

Al-Hallaj was killed but the extreme views for which he stood continued to live. Chief among these was existentialist monism (wahdat al-wujud), which drew upon Neoplatonic doctrines including the pseudo-Aristotelian theology. The first to formulate this theory was a Spanish Arab, Muhyi-al-Din ibn-'Arabi (1165–1240), the greatest mystic the Arabs produced and one of their greatest poets. When thirty-seven years old ibn-'Arabi left Seville for the East, never to return. After visiting Mecca, Baghdad, and Cairo he settled in Damascus. In his encyclopedic work (al-Futuhat al-Makkiyah, "the Meccan conquests") he gave a systematization of Sufism as he understood it, with the thesis that all being is essentially one, a manifestation of the divine substance. Things emanate from the divine essence, in which they

[2] Ibn-Khallikan, Wafayat al-A'yan (Cairo, 1299), vol. 1, p. 261. Cf. Philip K. Hitti, History of the Arabs, 10th ed. (New York and London, 1970), p. 436, and Reynold A. Nicholson, Studies in Islamic Mysticism (Cambridge, 1921), p. 80.

61

preexisted as ideas. Ibn-'Arabi was perhaps the first Sufi to use the term "the perfect man" (*al-insan al-kamil*), whom he defined as a microcosm in which are reflected all that is highest and best in the macrocosm. Muhammad, he taught, was not only the head of the prophetic hierarchy but a Logos of God. Sufis generally identify the perfect man with one who has achieved union with the divine.

Ibn-'Arabi's religious point of view went beyond the bounds of ecumenicism:

> My heart is capable of every form:
> A cloister for the monk, a fane for idols,
> a pasture for gazelles, the votary's Kaabah,
> the tables of the Torah, the Koran.
> Love is the creed I hold. Wherever turn
> its courses, love is still my creed and my faith.[3]

The Spanish mystic was undoubtedly the most influential one the Arabs produced. The impact of his teaching is manifest in Persian and Turkish followers. His theories of the Logos and of the perfect man are reflected in Jalal-al-Din al-Rumi's poetry, one of the glories of Persian literature.

Al-Rumi (1207–73) was born in Persia but flourished in Konia (Konieh, Quniyah) under the patronage of a Saljuq sultan. Asia Minor was then known as the "land of the Romans," from which his surname was taken. In his six-volume poetical masterpiece *Mathnawi* ("couplets"), on which he worked forty years, al-Rumi did for his people what ibn-'Arabi had done for his — he systemized all the concepts and theories of Sufism. In its stylistic beauty, the depth of its feeling, and the originality of its imagery and allegory the *Mathnawi* stands out as supreme among other Persian mystic works such as those by Sa'di, Hafiz, and Jami.

Al-Rumi shares with ibn-'Arabi theories of existentialist monism. He identifies himself with nature, following a system of transmigration, and rejoices not in a personal life continuing beyond the grave but in self-integration in the person of the Godhead:

> I died as a mineral and became a plant,
> I died as a plant and rose to animal,

[3] Cf. Reynold A. Nicholson, *A Literary History of the Arabs* (Cambridge, reprint 1966), p. 403.

I died as animal and I was man.
Why should I fear? When was I less by dying?
Yet once more I shall die as man, to soar
With angels blest; but even from angelhood
I must pass on: all except God doth perish.
When I have sacrificed my angel soul,
I shall become what no mind e'er conceived.
Oh, let me not exist! for Non-existence
Proclaims in organ tones, "To Him we shall return." [4]

Al-Rumi's admirers bestowed on him the honorific title of "Maw-lana" ("our master"). Hence he was the eponymous founder of the Mawlawi order. This was not the first Sufi fraternal order. Its members became known in the West as the whirling dervishes because of the ritualistic dances, accompanied by songs and music, which they practice. Such procedures were clearly contrary to the spirit and custom of orthodox Islam. Ritualistic dances characterized primitive religions and became part of the religion of Israel, as was made clear in the stories of Moses and David. The prophets cited in 1 Samuel 10:5 have been called Hebrew dervishes. But the Mawlawis consider their dances a means to attain ecstasy and a representation of the movement of heavenly bodies. The Mawlawi order spread in Turkey, Syria, and other lands. Its superior, always a descendant of the founder, enjoyed the privilege of girding each new Ottoman sultan-caliph with his sword. With the secularization of the state under Mustafa Kemal, this and other religious institutions were obliterated.

True, the loftiest flights in Moslem literature — whether Arabic, Persian, or Turkish — into spiritual space were undertaken on Sufi wings, but the sailing has never been smooth. Throughout its long development, culminating in ibn-'Arabi's and al-Rumi's productions, mystic literature has been characterized with vague symbolism and extravagant allegory. The language is as enigmatic as the mystery the mystics seek to solve. What counts is not the literal, the apparent — they say — but the inner, the esoteric. The "wine" the novice is encouraged to drink "that it may set him free from himself" is not the wine of grapes or dates but that of love. Some people hold that the world-renowned poet of wine and love 'Umar al-Khayyam was speaking

⁴ Reynold A. Nicholson, *The Mystics of Islam* (Beirut, reprint, 1966), p. 168.

of divine love and divine wine when he wrote (in the translation of
Edward Fitzgerald):

> A Book of Verses underneath the Bough,
> A Jug of Wine, a Loaf of Bread — and Thou
> Beside me singing in the Wilderness —
> O, Wilderness were Paradise enow.

Christian and Hebrew exegetes say the same about the songs ascribed
to Solomon.

III

FOR the first three centuries after its rise, Sufism was practiced individually or in small groups. It had no congregational features. Twelfth-cen-
tury Baghdad, the intellectual and political center of Islam, cradled
the earliest Sufi orders and provided them with a focal point from
which they could radiate in all directions. This was the time and place
in which triumphant Sufism started on its worldwide expansion. It was
to become a popular religion of Islam.

The earliest and most attractive Sufi order was al-Qadiri, named
after its founder, the Persian ʿAbd-al-Qadir al-Jili (al-Jilani, 1077–1166).
ʿAbd-al-Qadir started as a teacher-preacher and became so popular
that a special school building was erected for him by public subscrip-
tion. This became the "monastery" (*zawiyah*) for his order. His organization distinguished itself by its tolerant attitude and concern for the
welfare of the criminal and the poor. Its branches spread from Morocco to Java and many of them are still alive. The beautiful shrine of
the saint, built outside Baghdad by Sultan Sulayman the Magnificent,
is still a favorite place to visit in a city known as the "city of shrines."

The second fraternal order was founded in Baghdad too, by
Ahmad al-Rifaʿi (d. 1183) and named after him. Ahmad knew ʿAbd-
al-Qadir and some say he studied under him but his order later developed a strange feature: to impress people with their superhuman
power, adherents engaged in such fantastic deeds as glass-swallowing,
snake-handling, and passing needles and knives through their bodies.
Alien to Islam, such performances echo Hindu feats.

Various other orders and fraternities mushroomed over the area of
Islam and ranged in their Sufism from ascetic quietism to pantheistic

64

antinomianism. In practice as in doctrine, each order went its own way. Some encouraged and practiced celibacy, which is frowned upon in the Koran (24:32). By the end of the thirteenth century, Sufism and Arab intellectualism in general were on the decline. The supply of new ideas was almost exhausted. But orders continued to exist. What carried Islam to the millions east of India as far as the Philippines was not the soldier but the Sufi and the merchant. (Islam in that entire area, however, is marginal to this study and so will not be dealt with here.) Even in modern times new orders were still being born, especially in Africa. One of these, the Sanusi (1837), bears the name of an Algerian shaykh. The order had political and military as well as religious aims. It developed into a congregation-state, headed by the king of Libya until his deposition in 1969. Shi'ite Persia developed its own orders.

Normally an order begins its career in a cell or in a shaykh's home. As it grows it erects and endows its own zawiyah (or *takiyah*) through the generosity of the pious. The inmates of each zawiyah constitute a brotherhood, living, worshiping, and working together. Known as "dervishes" or "fakirs" (Ar. *faqir*, "poor," "beggar") they practice asceticism and meditation while going through a course of study prescribed by the shaykh. Solemn ceremonies initiate the novice and graduate the Sufi.

The central religious exercise is called *dhikr* ("remembrance and mention [of Allah's name]"), based on surah 33, verse 41: "O ye who believe, remember Allah with much remembrance and glorify Him morn and eve." The dhikr consists of incessant repetition of such a formula as *la ilaha illa Allah* in unison and in a monotonous voice, all synchronized with movements of the body. The collective effect may be described as hypnotic. Laymen may attach themselves to local orders and participate in such exercises when possible with no interruption to their normal work. They are similar to lay brothers in the Christian Church. The dhikr is the most elaborate Moslem ritual and suggests Christian litanies as a source.

In some dhikrs the repetitive formula is the excellent names of Allah. The rosary (*subhah*) is then used. Originally a Buddhistic instrument of worship, the rosary was borrowed by Eastern Christians and passed on to the Sufis. The Crusaders found it in the Middle East and introduced it into the West, where it is still used in Roman Catholic churches.

In most instances the order's founder is invested by his disciples and admirers with supernatural powers. Veneration leads to idolization and ends in sanctification. He is then honorifically known as *wali* ("friend [of Allah]") and becomes the center of a cult. The function of the wali, like that of the Christian saint, is mediation, and as in Christianity Moslem saints are organized in a hierarchy. Sufis consider themselves the select of Islam and their walis the select of the select. The wali is outranked by the Prophet and does not perform miracles (*mu'jizat*) as the Prophet does, but simply bestows miraculous gifts (*karamat*, cf. "gift of healing" in 1 Cor. 12:9). Nothing could have been more of an anathema to Islam than this doctrine of sainthood. Yet it was in due course so domesticated that today hardly a Moslem town from Morocco to Indonesia does not boast one or more saints represented by shrines.

IV

THE Sufis were fortunate in having produced a man to reconcile their views with orthodoxy and reinstate their rights as citizens of the community of Islam. Such a man had to be a master theologian, a consummate jurist, a profound philosopher, and an experienced mystic. The rare combination found a happy embodiment in the singular person of al-Ghazzali, one of the most engaging figures in the universal history of religious thought.

Abu-Hamid Muhammad al-Ghazzali (1058–1111) started his religious education as a boy under a Sufi shaykh in his birthplace Tus (eastern Persia). He continued it at the Nizamiyah of Naysabur where he studied theology and jurisprudence under one of the most learned scholars of the age, adding philosophy, logic, and natural science to his store of knowledge. Endowed with a sense of curiosity, a brilliant mind, and a photographic memory, abu-Hamid became the envy of his classmates and even aroused the jealousy of the professor he was asked to assist. From the Nizamiyah of Naysabur he moved on to the Nizamiyah of Baghdad to occupy the chair of theology and enjoy the patronage of the enlightened Persian vizir Nizam-al-Mulk in the Saljuq court of the capital. This vizir had founded and endowed in Baghdad the academy bearing his name, which he envisioned as a model to be emulated throughout the realm. The thirty-three-year-old professor dwarfed his colleagues as he had dwarfed his classmates. Students and established scholars were drawn from near and far to study or consult with him. Even the Berber founder of the Murabit (Almoravid) dynasty in Morocco and Spain sought his counsel on a legal problem.

The new post and patronage brought him honor, power, fame, and money but not peace of mind. Intellectualism failed to satisfy him. Traditional beliefs lost their authority for him. His mind roved through the whole spiritual-intellectual spectrum of the age:

> Ever since I was twenty (I am now over fifty) . . . I have not ceased to investigate every dogma I come across. No esoteric did I meet without desiring to investigate his esotericism; no philosopher, without wanting to learn the essence of his philosophy; no dialectical theologian, without striving to ascertain the object of his dialectics and theology; no Sufi, without longing to probe the secret of his asceticism; no atheist, without groping for the reasons of his atheism. Such was the unquenchable thirst of my soul for research from my youth — an instinct and a temperament implanted in me by Allah through no choice of mine.[5]

When he suffered what is called today a nervous breakdown, the thirty-nine-year-old man resigned his post, turned his back on civilization, left his family, and roamed from place to place. Dressed as a poor dervish, he entered Damascus and went into retreat in its Umayyad Mosque. Every morning — he tells us in his *al-Munqidh min al-Dalal* ("the deliverer from error") — he would climb its minaret, shut the door behind him, and spend the day in prayer, contemplation, and writing. The minaret is still shown to visitors to the Syrian capital. The product of his work was his masterpiece *Ihya 'Ulum al-Din* ("the revivification of the sciences of religion") which according to a later student of theology would in itself suffice if all other works on theology were destroyed. From Damascus the dervish made trips to Jerusalem, Mecca, Medina, and other holy places.

[5] Al-Ghazzali, *Al-Munkidh min al-Dalal*, ed. 'Abd-al-Halim Hahmud (Damascus, 1385), pp. 70–1. Cf. Philip K. Hitti, *Makers of Arab History* (New York and London, 1968), pp. 145, 150.

After a decade of alienation a new al-Ghazzali, restored in health and reintegrated in personality, returned to his home and family. The transformation, in his own words in the autobiographical section of *al-Munqidh*, was brought about "not by proof or argument but by a light put in my heart by Allah, the light that is the key to real knowledge." But on his return he considered neither Baghdad nor Naysabur the appropriate locale for his new teaching. In his native Tus he established a zawiyah to commune individually with the seekers of truth and to indulge in his favorite way of life. But time was not generous. On December 18, 1111 — to borrow the words of an Arab biographer of learned men — "Allah withdrew the gift He had bestowed, calling it back to the glory of His presence." Al-Ghazzali's life was unquestionably one of the noblest in the annals of Islam.

Generally considered the greatest theologian of Islam, al-Ghazzali is mentioned here only in the context of his contribution to philosophy and Sufism. In his critique *Tahafut al-Falasifah* ("the inconsistencies of philosophers") he worked out twenty points of conflict between philosophic thought and Islam. Greek philosophy was then familiar through Arabic translations by Syrian Christians. He denied that philosophic thought could form a valid basis for religious life; that was entirely a question of personal experience, he claimed. But the Moslem theologian acknowledged and himself used Aristotelian logic. He saw no contradiction between mathematics (then a branch of philosophy) and the teachings of Islam. He accepted the doctrines of divine light and of the dichotomy between soul and body which were current in Neoplatonism. What he appropriated from philosophy was incorporated into Moslem theology and remains there as a fixture. He moreover dissipated the mystery surrounding philosophy, making it look equivalent to rational thinking and within the range of the ordinary mind. Thus philosophic thinking was assured a permanent place in Islam.

More extensive and profound was al-Ghazzali's contribution in the Sufi field. Thanks to his writings and example mysticism became a respectable form of Islamic piety. As a result of his influence love came to play a more important role in the worshiper-worshiped relationship. (Incidentally this Moslem Sufi frequently quotes 'Isa [Jesus] but the quotations are largely apocryphal or inaccurate.) That personal experience could be a valid proof of God's existence was established in orthodoxy. Even chants and music, after the restrictions al-Ghazzali imposed on them, became tolerable.

The impact of al-Ghazzali's mystic teachings was not limited to the world of Islam. It left noticeable traces in Christian and Jewish thinking in the East as well as in the West, where he became known as Algazel. In less than forty years after his death, part of his work had been translated into Latin. Dante used his name; Thomas Aquinas and other scholastic scholars used his works, as did ibn-Maymun (Maimonides), the celebrated Jewish philosopher of medieval times.

Through al-Ghazzali and media that transmitted his ideas Sufism established itself as the distinctive contribution of Islam to ecumenical thought.

الجزء الثاني : الاسلام كدولة

PART II *Islam the State*

THE CALIPHAL STATE
IN MEDINA AND DAMASCUS

❖❖ AT THE beginning of the rise of Islam the two world powers were
the Byzantine or East Roman Empire and the Persian Empire. One
was Christian and the other Zoroastrian. It was truly startling that a new
power, preaching a strange religion, emerged from little-known Arabia, stripped one of the two empires of its richest provinces in Asia
and Africa, and destroyed the other to its very foundation. By 642, ten
years after the death of the Prophet, the Persian Empire had been
erased from the register of existence, and the Byzantine Empire had
lost greater Syria (from the Taurus to Sinai) and Egypt. How and
why this astounding episode came about is one of the most fascinating
stories of medieval times.

I

CLEARLY Muhammad was not directly involved. The conquests were
all achieved after his death. In his lifetime Islam's political control did
not extend far beyond Hijaz. Tribes to the north and south, including
Christian Najran, had signed peace treaties with him, but beyond that
Muhammad probably exercised no effective control. It will be recalled
that even Mecca did not acknowledge him until a couple of years before his death. He did, however, establish the precedent that politics
and force were not incompatible with the precepts of Islam.

Nor did abu-Bakr, his father-in-law and first successor (caliph, 632–4), have much to do with any but the initial conquests. Muhammad appointed no successor. As caliph, abu-Bakr, a cloth merchant who was an early believer, succeeded to all but Muhammad's prophetic function. (As the last of the prophets, Muhammad could have no successor.) Abu-Bakr was not exactly elected to this high office. Rather, he was declared caliph by the elders of Medina, which was the capital, in a simple ceremony (*bay'ah*, "sale") involving clasping his hand as a sign of obedience. Obedience to the caliph, according to Islamic political theory, is tantamount to obedience to the Prophet, which in turn is equivalent to obedience to Allah. A crime against the state is then a sin against God. In Islam, no less than in Judaism and Christianity, the origin of government is divine and all authority derives from God. The only justification for a state is God's will.

The great task confronting the first caliph was not to bring back into the fold of Islam the Arabians of the southern and eastern parts of the peninsula (as some early historians assert) but to extend for the first time Islam's sway to those distant regions. The aged caliph was determined to carry out this task. If Islam could not conquer and bring under its control all Arabians, it could not hope to extend its influence to other countries, he reasoned.

The hero of these early campaigns was young Khalid ibn-al-Walid. In a few months his brilliant generalship won the tribes of southern, central, and eastern Arabia. The peninsula was for the first time in its history united under one man through the sword of Khalid. He then established his initial claim to the title "sword of Islam."

The military momentum thus acquired had to seek an outlet. The martial spirit of the tribes — now presumably forming a religious fraternity — had to find new channels of expression. The year before abu-Bakr's death two columns set out to march northward, one toward Iraq and Persia and the other toward Palestine and Syria. Khalid, who first commanded the eastern column, was ordered to rush to the aid of his coreligionists in the west who were being hard pressed by the Byzantine army. His perilous dash through the five-hundred-mile waterless desert in eighteen days became a saga of Arabic military literature. Unexpectedly Khalid appeared before the walls of the provincial

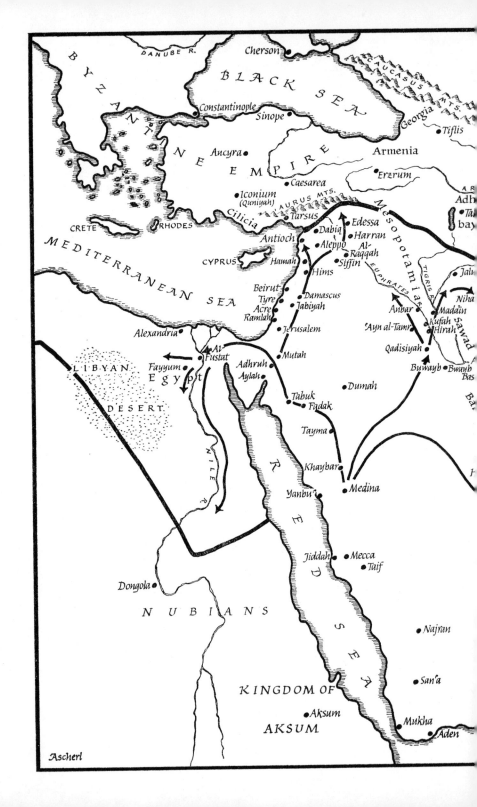

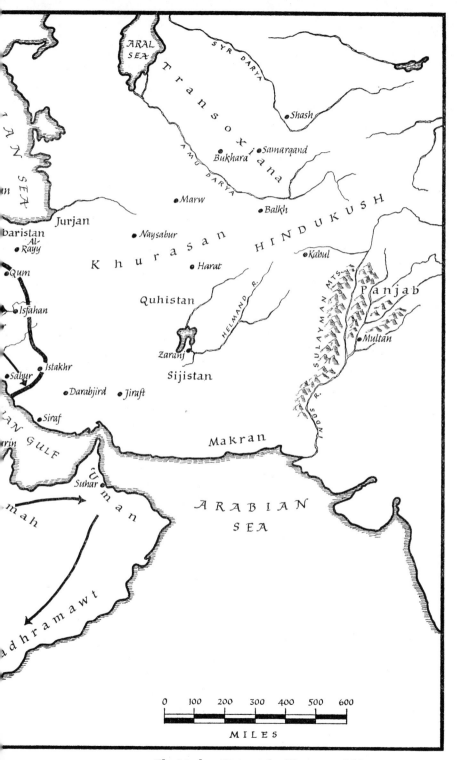

The Moslem State under 'Umar, ca. 644

capital, Damascus. A six months' siege of the city ended in its surrender to Khalid, but mainly because of treachery on the part of local officials headed by an ancestor of Saint John of Damascus. The terms of the treaty were simple and served as a future model: they involved a pledge of security on the part of the conqueror and an offer of tribute on the part of the conquered.

The decisive encounter was yet to come. On a hot August day in 636 the two armies stood face to face on the banks of the Yarmuk, the eastern tributary of the Jordan. The Byzantine army comprised about fifty thousand troops, mostly Armenian, Syrian, and Arab mercenaries. It was led by Theodorus, brother of the reigning emperor Heraclius. The Arab army — if it could be called that — numbered half as many. But the victory was Allah's. The way was opened for the conquest of the rest of Syria. The first country was thus added to the rising empire.

From Syria, the Moslems proceeded to new victories in Armenia and Egypt. The hero of the Egyptian campaign was another Qurayshite, 'Amr ibn-al-'As, Khalid's peer in dash and valor. Abu-Bakr's successor, 'Umar ibn-al-Khattab (634–44), halfheartedly authorized 'Amr to undertake the campaign. Like his predecessor, 'Umar was a merchant, but being more military minded than abu-Bakr, he assumed the new title *amir al-mu'minin* ("commander of the believers"), which became a synonym for "caliph." At the head of four thousand men, later augmented, 'Amr crossed the Syrian-Egyptian border and laid siege to Babylon, the border fortress near the site of modern Cairo. Being Christians the Egyptians were offered the usual three choices: tribute, Islam, or the sword. Cyrus, Byzantine governor and church patriarch, did not take the offer seriously. The city, considered impregnable by virtue of its double wall and moat, a fifty-thousand-man garrison, and a mighty fleet, yielded (640) to desert invaders with not a single ship, no siege machinery, and no immediate source of supply. The terms followed those given Damascus. The capture of the fortress left no obstacle all the way to the provincial capital at Alexandria. The occupation of the Nile valley opened the way for conquering North Africa and establishing contact with a new culture, the Berber.

Meanwhile trouble was erupting on the eastern front. Khalid's successor Sa'd ibn-abi-Waqqas, a Companion of the Prophet, had had

76

his first encounter with the Persian army at al-Qadisiyah, east of the Euphrates, and scored as sound a victory as any preliminary one by his coreligionists. From there he pushed across the two rivers to the imperial capital at Ctesiphon (al-Mada'in). The proud capital of western Asia and rival of Byzantium opened its doors (June 637) with hardly any resistance. Five years later with the fall of Nihawand the entire country was overrun. In 651 the fugitive Sasanid emperor Yazdagird was killed while fleeing, by one of his subjects who coveted the crown treasures he was carrying. An empire that had lasted for over a thousand years thus came to an ignominious end. Islam had its first contact with two new cultures — the Berber, mostly nomads who were cousins of the Semites, and the Indo-Iranian, which was destined to play a leading role in future events.

Arab historians, mostly theologians, explained all these phenomenal conquests in a way similar to the Old Testament's explanation of Hebrew conquests: it was all Providential. The term they used for the conquests was *fath* ("opening [the way for Islam]"); but for battles they used the term *ghazwahs* ("razzias," "raids"), the same term used for tribal forays aimed at booty. In fact what triumphed in these early conquests was not so much Islam the religion as Islam the nation-state Muhammad founded. It was Arabianism. The Islamization of the conquered peoples had to wait for a couple of centuries. On several earlier occasions the population of the barren Arabian peninsula, surrounded by water on three sides, had reached a point necessitating an outburst into the Fertile Crescent in quest of a richer life. This time, however, religion provided the spark that ignited the nationalistic powder keg.

The Byzantines and Persians — enfeebled by centuries of internecine wars and grown soft by luxurious living — seemed anemic if not effeminate before the Bedouin invaders, who were driven from an inhospitable, crowded habitat and emboldened by the promise of Paradise for those who fall in the "path of Allah." Religious factors facilitated the advance in its early stage. Some Arabian tribes on the Syrian and Persian frontiers were already domesticated from having lived a long time under Christian rule. The Syrians, Iraqis, and Egyptians, it should be added, belonged to Christian sects considered heretic by the official Byzantine Church (indeed, there were times in which these

Eastern Christians were subjected to persecution by their Byzantine masters), and to them Islam may have looked like a new Christian sect. Then there was the ethnic factor. Being Semites the Syrians and Iraqis must have felt closer to the Arabians than to the Byzantines. Not only in Damascus but in other towns as well natives welcomed the invaders and hoped for better times.

Some Arab historians maintain that the campaigns were conducted in accordance with preconceived, prearranged plans. Nothing could have been further from the truth. The creation of the Arab empire was due less to design than to the logic of impelling circumstances. Neither abu-Bakr nor 'Umar could have foreseen the ultimate course of events that was shaped under their very eyes but not entirely under their control. 'Umar, in whose reign the bulk of the conquests took place, repeatedly directed his generals not to let the sea intervene between them and him. He insisted that his troops occupy camps (rather than live in the cities) and stay mobile; thus Kufah and Basrah in Iraq and al-Fustat (later incorporated into Cairo) came to be.

What is remarkable about the Arab conquests is not only the rapidity and the orderly fashion with which they were achieved — with little wanton destruction — but the ease with which transition was made from war to peace, from conquest to administration. The Prophet's government was a one-man affair with no specialized bureaus, officials, or other trappings of large governments. One would search in vain in the thousands of Prophetic traditions for detailed instructions about governing. Abu-Bakr's government was tribal and patriarchal, for there were no patterns available to him for setting up a royal or imperial government. The problem then of administering a hastily assembled, far-flung empire with a multiplicity of languages, religions, and ethnic elements first arose during the reign of the second caliph. 'Umar followed the line of least resistance. He left virtually intact the Byzantine framework of provincial government in Syria and Egypt as well as the Sasanid administrative machinery in Persia, and tried to incorporate in it whatever Islamic-Arabian theories he had. Old functionaries and bureaucrats were left in their positions; they could not be replaced. The military register he instituted was of Persian origin as indicated by its designation (*diwan*). The language of the military and financial registers remained Greek in Damascus and Persian in Ctesiphon until early in the eighth century. 'Umar established the judiciary system in Islam and appointed the first judges to preside over the provinces. Evidently the caliph proceeded on the political theory that in the Arabian peninsula none but Moslems should be tolerated, that the Arabians abroad should remain a distinct religio-military community, that the conquered peoples should be left undisturbed in their varied professions and land cultivation, and that the Christians and Jews (sing. *dhimmi*, "covenant-protected") should be subject to heavy tribute but not to military duty. This put Arabian Moslems on the top of the sociopolitical ladder, with the Neo-Moslems next, the dhimmis one rung below, and the slaves and prisoners of war at the bottom.

Abu-Bakr and 'Umar initiated the orthodox caliphate, based in Medina. Their successors 'Uthman ibn-'Affan (644–56) and 'Ali ibn-abi-Talib (656–61) carried it forward. All four were Qurayshites; three were related by marriage to the Prophet. The murder of 'Ali in 661, following a period of struggle for the caliphate, marked the end of one era and the beginning of another. The change was not only political, but also cultural and social. The new era was inaugurated by Mu-'awiyah (661–80), founder of the Umayyad dynasty in Damascus.

II

MU'AWIYAH began his career as an officer in the army which conquered Syria; he then became its governor. His first task as governor was to reorganize the military. He changed the army from one organized in tribal units, each under its own shaykh, into a "modernized" one — disciplined, well paid, and modeled after the Byzantine army. Finding shipyards (*dar al-sina'ah*, from which is derived "arsenal") along the coast, he built the first navy in Islam and became its admiral (from Ar. *amir al-bahr*, "commander of the sea"). He could count on the full loyalty of his Syrian subjects partly because his wife, his physician, and his poet were Christians. In Damascus Islam began to breathe more of the Mediterranean and less of the desert.

Mu'awiyah outmaneuvered 'Ali, tactfully contested the caliphate with him, and was proclaimed by his Syrian followers caliph even be-

79

fore his rival's death. But this upstart was none other than the son of abu-Sufyan, archenemy of the Prophet and chief of the aristocratic Umayyad branch of the Quraysh. Hijaz and Iraq were obviously pro-'Alid; Egypt was partly so. But Mu'awiyah, regarded by Arab historians as one of the four political geniuses of Islam, was the man of the hour. His philosophy of rule he summed up thus: "I apply not my lash where my tongue suffices, nor my sword where the whip is enough. And if there be one hair binding me to my fellow men, I let it not break. If they pull I loosen, and if they loosen I pull." [1] Sensing that 'Ali's eldest son, al-Hasan, was more interested in the harem than in administration, he sent him what amounted to a blank check for him to fill out. He dispatched his friend 'Amr ibn-al-'As to reconquer Egypt for the new cause. His other lieutenants had no difficulty in doing the same in Iraq and Persia.

The military machine whose operation after the first two caliphs had been interrupted by the civil war was reactivated. For the first time, in 668, the Moslems indulged in the daydream of capturing Constantinople, the haughty and mighty Christian capital. But the rigors of a severe winter turned out to be a greater enemy. The campaign, led by Yazid, the caliph's son by his Christian wife, proved to be a failure. Yazid had by then been appointed crown prince, a procedure without precedent in Islam. Mu'awiyah must have sensed the advantage in stability to the state from such procedure. Yazid distinguished himself by becoming the first in a long line of drunkard caliphs.

Six years later the armored arm of the caliph in Damascus again stretched all the way to the capital of the eternal enemy. This time naval forces cooperated with land forces. The seven-year siege ended in failure. One reason was the use the Christians made of the so-called Greek fire, a highly combustible compound that could burn on and under water. Eight centuries had to pass before the city on the Bosporus would yield to a Moslem invader — Ottoman Turkish, though, rather than Arab.

The more southerly thrust through Byzantine North Africa was more productive of results. Using Egypt as a base, Mu'awiyah's lieu-

[1] Al-Ya'qubi, Ta'rikh, ed. M. Th. Houtsma (Leyden, 1883), vol. 2, p. 265. Cf. Philip K. Hitti, History of Syria Including Lebanon and Palestine, 2nd ed. (New York and London, 1957), p. 439.

tenants carried the banner of Islam triumphantly over present-day Libya and Tunisia. One of them built in 670 al-Qayrawan (Kairouan, "caravan stopping place"). The city developed into a leading military and cultural center in Africa, a successor of Carthage, not far from whose site it was built. To Western Moslems it became the city that ranked fourth in importance after Mecca, Medina, and Jerusalem. From al-Qayrawan Arab troops reinforced by Berbers ultimately chased the Byzantines out of the entire continent.

More difficult was the task of reconquering, pacifying, and consolidating the regions to the east: Iraq was a hotbed of Shi'sm; Persia cherished a proud memory of nationalism and imperialism and an equally proud tradition of cultural achievement. But Mu'awiyah's viceroy, stationed at Basrah, measured up to the responsibility. Not satisfied with possessing only the Iranian territory, he and his successors crossed over into the Turkish-speaking domain. In 674 their troops penetrated Transoxiana, captured Bukhara, and pushed into Samarqand and other cities which in due course became brilliant centers of Islamic culture. Thus was the Arab brought into direct contact with not only a new ethnic group — the Turkish, related to the Mongolian — but a new religion — Buddhism. And when the arm holding the sword of Islam became paralyzed it was the Ottoman Turks who caught and wielded it effectively. The varied Turkish, Mongol, and other Moslem states which arose in central Asia, India, and farther east, however, will not be considered in this study.

Arab historians did not consider Mu'awiyah the hero that he was. To the Shi'ites among them he was a prime enemy: not only did he wrest the caliphate from its legitimate holder, but he passed it on to his progeny. An integral part of their prayer involved invoking Allah's curse on him and his successor Yazid, who was responsible for the murder of 'Ali's second son, al-Husayn. To the Sunnite historians, mostly working in the hostile 'Abbasid atmosphere, the first Umayyad caliph was a late believer; his conversion was more a matter of convenience than of conviction. Priority in accepting Islam determined the hierarchy. Moreover he changed the headship of Islam from caliphal to royal and installed himself as the first king, called *malik*, a despicable title to the Arabs in those days. Among other innovations he surrounded himself with a bodyguard and erected a throne in his palace and a bower for his private use in the mosque.

The fact, however, remains that if he is judged by achievement, Mu'awiyah stands out after Muhammad and 'Umar as third greatest in Arab history. He modernized the state and made it an empire. Many of his successors tried to emulate the model he set in energy, tolerance, and *finesse politique* — but few succeeded.

III

THE dynasty inaugurated by Mu'awiyah reached its zenith in power, glory, and affluence in the rule of his sixth successor, 'Abd-al-Malik (685–705), and his son al-Walid (705–15). It was during their reigns that the Arabization of the state was completed: the language of the bureaus of registry was changed to Arabic, as was the coinage. It was then that the grand Umayyad Mosque in Damascus was built to take its place as the fourth sanctuary in the Eastern Islam. Construction of the third, the Dome of the Rock in Jerusalem, was started by 'Abd-al-Malik on the site of the rock where Muhammad on his nocturnal journey ascended to heaven. The architects of these monumental structures were Syrians of the Byzantine school. The Syrian Moslem could then worship in as sumptuous a place as any cathedral of the area in which a Christian could worship.

In this period imperial expansion reached its farthest point eastward. The entire area in central Asia and western India (Pakistan today) was Islamized, and so it remained. The same was true of North Africa, where Berbers were not only Islamized but partially Arabicized. Here in a few years Arabs achieved what neither Romans nor Byzantines in centuries were able to achieve.

When at last the victorious march of Islam reached the Atlantic it was deflected northward. In 711 a Berber ex-slave, Tariq, at the head of seven thousand troops crossed the narrow straits and immortalized his name in Gibraltar (Jabal ["mount of"] Tariq). In six short years the Iberian peninsula was overrun; the first European territory was annexed by Islam. In 918 the Pyrenees were crossed. Not until Tours (in northwestern France) was reached did the march come to a halt. The

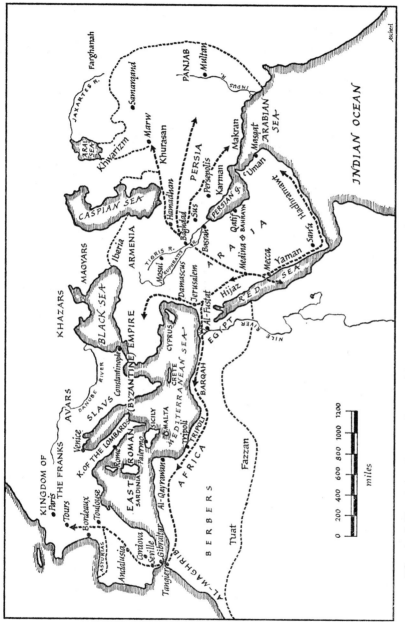

The Arab Empire at Its Height, ca. 750

halt was due more to natural causes than to the generalship of Charles Martel, commander of the Frankish army. The invaders, thousands of miles from their base, unfamiliar with the terrain, and unprepared for the onslaught of cold weather, simply reached a standstill and called a retreat. This was the extent of the victory hailed by Western historians as one of the decisive battles of history. They, including Edward Gibbon, father of English history, envisioned Paris and London with mosques where cathedrals now stand, and with men wearing fezzes rather than hats, had the outcome been otherwise.

The year of the battle (732), however, is a convenient date from which to take stock, especially since it marks the first centennial of Muhammad's death. Thus the followers of the Arabian Prophet, a hundred years after his death, found themselves masters of an empire larger than that of Rome at its greatest.

By now the varied functions of the government — political, military, judicial, financial, and executive — had become more clearly differentiated and defined. The caliph, with the title *amir al-mu'minin* was, of course, the undisputed head. He appointed the provincial governments and held them responsible for the political and military administration of their respective provinces. At times he appointed even the tax collectors. Gradually he delegated more authority to his governors to appoint tax collectors and judges. Judges and theologians were responsible for the religious life of the community. Dhimmis remained under the jurisdiction of their denominations' heads, who handled not only personal status cases but civil and criminal cases involving their followers, too. Adherents of other than Christianity and Judaism were now treated as if they were included in the dhimmi category.

Moslem Arabians, headed by the Umayyad house, constituted the aristocracy of the state. They specialized in governmental and military affairs, leaving industry, trade, agriculture, and the professions to natives. Those natives who embraced Islam were disappointed to find themselves in a lower social class than Arabian Moslems. Even when they became Moslems and placed themselves under the protection of Arabian tribes, they remained second-class citizens. This was the more galling because they were conscious of the higher culture they represented. No wonder they later appear in history as singularly disposed

84

to espouse all kinds of doctrines heretical to religion and inimical to the state.

IV

AFTER al-Walid the caliphate started on its precipitous course downward. The course was slippery and the distance short. Hardly any of al-Walid's successors were worthy of the heritage. Most of them were inept, if not dissolute or degenerate. Their courts featured slave singers, boon companions, fun dealers, and other pleasure peddlers. Against the vices of civilization the sons of the desert had developed no immunity. To the sudden increase in wealth were added a superabundance of slaves and the concubine system picked up from the conquered area. That made indulgence in luxury the rule of the day. Clearly the regime was engaged in self-destruction before it was engaged in battle with an enemy intent on its destruction.

Among the potential enemies were dissatisfied Neo-Moslems and clients in all the provinces, particularly Persia. Then there were the dissident Shi'ites, with whom Iraq was seething. Shi'ites viewed the Damascus caliphs as ungodly usurpers to be overthrown at the earliest possible opportunity. Even certain Sunnite pietists, . impressed by Umayyad worldliness, sympathized with the 'Abbasid and 'Alid cause. The explosive elements were there waiting for someone to ignite them.

The spark was provided by a Qurayshite, abu-al-'Abbas, scion of a first cousin of the Prophet. His credentials were closer blood connection and earlier religious relationship to Muhammad than the Umayyad caliph could claim. His platform was to return the caliphate to orthodoxy and to provide satisfaction to anti-Umayyad parties. His plan was to unite all opposition under his leadership. The 'Abbasid propaganda had been skillfully distributed underground for years.

Abu-al-'Abbas led the Iraqi revolution from his headquarters in Kufah. It was in that city's mosque, in November 749, that homage was paid to him publicly as caliph. In the meantime his emissary abu-Muslim al-Khurasani, a Persian ex-slave, had won his country over to the new cause and routed the Umayyad garrisons. Everywhere, even in Syria, the white banner of the Umayyads was in retreat before the black banner of the 'Abbasids (black was supposedly the color of the

Prophet's banner) and the green of the 'Alids. Events moved to a climax. The final encounter took place on a tributary of the Tigris in January 750. Loyal Syrian troops, numbering twelve thousand and led by the caliph himself, Marwan II (744–50), were utterly destroyed. The fugitive commander was pursued to Egypt, caught hiding in a church, and decapitated. His head was sent to abu-al-'Abbas in Kufah. Marwan was the fourteenth and last caliph of the Umayyad line.

The Syrian capital opened its gates to the invaders after a brief siege. Its caliphal tombs were desecrated and their contents exhumed; even the dead were punished. As for the living the punishment was extermination — by covert if not by overt means. An invitation to a banquet was tendered to the male members of the fallen house. Accepting it on its face value some eighty princes responded. The meeting place was near Jaffa. As they started eating, the guests were treacherously attacked by the hosts and mercilessly cut down. Leather covers were spread over the victims and the executioners continued their meal to the accompaniment of human groans. Waiting hungry dogs were allowed to feast on the corpses.

Thus was written in red ink the last chapter of one Moslem state and the first of another.

THE CALIPHAL STATE IN BAGHDAD

❖❖ THE shift from an Umayyad to an 'Abbasid regime was more than a
dynastic change. It had geographic, ethnic, socioeconomic, and political aspects. Iraq moved to the forefront as Syria receded to the background; the orientation became toward Persia. The Arab aristocracy
that had been in control was gradually replaced by a multi-ethnic
group called Arab, in the sense of Arab-speaking, but including Neo-
Moslems and clients — mostly Persians, who were under the protection
of various Arabian tribes. As the military caste was deposed the preoc-
cupation of the government turned from warfare to trade and industry. Gradually pensions paid to Arabian warriors ceased. Arabs rather
than Arabians became the spearhead of Islam.

The 'Abbasid regime made its debut under false pretenses. Its victory, it claimed, was over a non-Moslem state — a secular one — which
was to be replaced by a true caliphate. In fact the 'Abbasids feigned
religiosity, seeking religion for its cohesive rather than its spiritual
properties. The record does not show that they were less worldly than
the ones they overthrew. Far from making the state subordinate to
Islam, they used Islam to give the state legitimacy and respectability.

I

IN HIS inaugural speech at the Kufah mosque, abu-al-'Abbas bestowed
upon himself the honorific title of *al-saffah* ("the bloodshedder"). He

thereafter did his best to live up to the title, and it became his second name. The state executioner took his place near the throne. In contrast to Mu'awiyah, abu-al-'Abbas al-Saffah bequeathed to his successors a tradition of violence.

One of the first acts of his brother al-Mansur (754–75) was to invite the regime's friend and supporter abu-Muslim al-Khurasani, the powerful governor of Khurasan, to an audience in his palace, where he treacherously disposed of him. The turn of the Shi'ite allies came next. These had naïvely thought the 'Abbasids were fighting their battle. The leaders of their uprisings in Kufah, Medina, and other places were tracked down and eliminated. Other troublemakers were Umayyad sympathizers with whom the first 'Abbasid caliphs had to deal.

Al-Mansur, rather than al-Saffah, was the true founder of the dynasty. All thirty-five successors were his lineal descendants. He was also the founder of the 'Abbasid capital of Baghdad on the west bank of the Tigris and next door to Ctesiphon, the Chosroes's capital. Circular in form and defended by a double wall and a wide moat, the new city was centered on the caliphal palace, adjoined by the congregational mosque. The palace was conspicuous by its green dome and golden gate. Gradually the Baghdad court became more Persian than the Damascus court was Syrian.

In the new court a new office developed, the vizirate. Its first incumbent was a Persian of Buddhist origin, Khalid al-Barmaki. Khalid served as caliphal counselor, chief executive, and state treasurer. He was succeeded in this high office by his descendants. The Barmakis amassed fabulous fortunes, entertained royally, gave lavishly to friends and well-wishers, and gained a measure of popularity that eclipsed the caliph's. In 803 al-Mansur's grandson Harun al-Rashid extinguished the upstarts. The severed head of his Barmaki vizir was impaled on one of Baghdad's bridges; the halves of his bisected body were exhibited on the two other bridges. In Harun's firmament there could not be two suns. The Barmaki family was then wiped out of existence, but the name has survived in an Arabic proverb: as generous as a Barmaki.

The governmental machinery in Baghdad became more complicated and better organized. The caliph now had a chancellor for official correspondence and also a chamberlain for introducing high officials and foreign envoys. His vizir — in reality grand vizir — served as his chief executive and presided over the council of state. A leading member of the council was the head of the bureau of taxes. Finances remained a main concern of the state. A chief source of revenue was the zakah, collected from believers and dispersed for the benefit of the needy among them. A richer and more copious source was the capitation and land taxes raised from non-Moslems and applied to paying the salaries of troops and government officials and to financing roads, bridges, and public structures. The annual land tax income from the provinces — exclusive of taxes paid in kind — reached the high figure of 331,929,068 dirhams under Harun's son al-Ma'mun.

The earlier provincial organization of the empire was not radically altered. In theory the governor held his position at the pleasure of the vizir, and behind the vizir, the caliph. But in all local affairs the governor tended to become supreme and his office hereditary. The increase in his authority over the judiciary and taxation varied in direct proportion to his personal ability, caliphal weakness, and distance from the imperial capital.

An interesting development in the judiciary was the institution of a bureau for inspection of grievances. It was evidently introduced by al-Mahdi, the son and successor of al-Mansur. Intended to set aright cases of miscarriage of justice, this bureau served as a court of appeal and handled cases involving the administrative and political departments. The Umayyad caliphs, beginning with 'Abd-al-Malik (d. 705), handled such cases personally at specified times each week.

Another innovation, related to the police department, appeared in the days of al-Ma'mun. A municipal police officer titled *muhtasib* ("calculator") functioned as the overseer of markets and public morals. He saw to it that proper weights and measures were used and that such illegal acts as gambling, usury, and the public sale of wine were not committed. Maintenance of the recognized standards of morality between the sexes was added to his duties. The institution survived in Persia, Moslem India, and other successor states of the caliphate until the nineteenth century.

Postal service, inaugurated by Mu'awiyah, was further developed by Harun and his successors. Primarily designed to serve state interests, the institution began to handle private correspondence. Relays of mules and horses covered the routes linking the caliphal with the provincial capitals. The postmaster general served simultaneously as the chief of the espionage system. As such he was the inspector general and confidential agent of the central government.

The 'Abbasid caliphate, most celebrated and longest-lived (750–1258) in Islam, reached the apogee of its might and affluence under the fifth caliph, Harun al-Rashid (786–809), and his son al-Ma'-mun (813–33). History and legend have collaborated to make this period the golden prime of the entire Arab caliphate. Through the *Arabian Nights* Harun's name has become a part of the heritage of the civilized world. The legendary Harun, however, dwarfs the historical one. In Arab tradition this caliph was the *beau idéal* of Moslem royalty. His munificence, his patronage of art and literature, his style of conduct and living became proverbial. Harun's court served as a model even as far away as Morocco and Moslem Spain. As a magnet it attracted poets, belletrists, musicians, artists, dancers, and singers from all over the realm. The caliph with his harem, eunuchs, and officials occupied a third of the round city. Zubaydah, a cousin and wife of the caliph, set the fashion for dress among the aristocracy. In 825 when al-Ma'mun was married, the bridal couple was showered with a thousand large pearls. The guests each received a gift of an estate or a slave.

Luxurious living characterized other than royalty and aristocracy. A new middle class of merchants, craftsmen, and professionals emerged in this and the following century. It created and shared the new wealth. Baghdad developed as the leading domestic and foreign trade and industrial center. A network of land and sea routes linked it to the prominent centers of the empire and of the outside world. Eastward, Moslem traders reached China; northward they penetrated Russia; westward they halted on the Atlantic shores. The chief attraction in China was silk. The "great silk way" led through Transoxiana and Turkestan, noted for their furs, felt cloaks, and other woolen products. Persia supplied rugs and embroidered goods. India and South Arabia yielded spices. Syria offered the international market inlaid woodwork and the time-honored glass of Sidon and Tyre. Not least among the commodities sought in non-Moslem markets was the human commodity — slaves. The reduction in foreign wars at this time had, however, dammed a main source of this supply.

The chronicles of the day cite cases of industrial magnates and business tycoons with fortunes reminiscent of the Rockefellers' and the Rothschilds' of our day. A Basran marine merchant had an annual income of a million dirhams; a Baghdad jeweler remained wealthy after a caliph had confiscated sixteen million dinars of his fortune.

II

BUT the true glory of the period lies in its cultural achievements. Under al-Ma'mun (813–33) one of the most significant movements in the history of Moslem thought began.

The first stage of the new intellectual era was characterized by the translation of works of various origins into Arabic. It was initiated by the rendition into Arabic of a Hindi treatise on astronomy, introducing this science to the Moslem world, and with it the numerals designated by the Arabs as Hindi and by the Europeans as Arabic. A scientist under al-Ma'mun's patronage, al-Khwarizmi (d. ca. 850), utilized the new material to work out the first astronomical tables in Arabic. He also used the new numerical system in his tables and in his book on algebra.

From Persian the earliest short stories came into Arabic in the form of fables designed to teach lessons of proper conduct through the experience of animals. The fables were by an Indian philosopher named Bidpai and were originally written in Hindi. However, both the Persian and Hindi versions were eventually lost and the Arabic served as the origin for translations into some forty European and Asian languages. (The French fabulist La Fontaine acknowledged his indebtedness to the Bidpai fables.)

Immeasurably richer than the Persian or the Hindi was the Hellenic source. It was this source that supplied Islam with its philosophic concepts and scientific thought. The intermediary was Christian Syria, whose scholars had for centuries used Greek. The dean of translators was a Nestorian, Hunayn ibn-Ishaq (809–73). The Hunayn school was

91

responsible for making accessible to the Arabic reader the philosophical masterpieces of Aristotle and Plato, together with the medical works of Hippocrates and Galen and the botany of Dioscorides. Hunayn headed an interesting foundation named House of Wisdom, which was established by al-Ma'mun (830) as a combination library, academy, and translation bureau. The caliph's interest stemmed from his radical views and espousal of the Mu'tazilite doctrine. In quest of material in support of his new beliefs he sent emissaries to Constantinople and, it is said, to Sicily.

In addition to the Hunayn school of translators, Syria provided a Harranian school headed by Thabit ibn-Qurrah (836–901). Harran was a center of star worship and its scholars specialized in astronomical and geographical works. Thanks to Thabit and his pupils the masterpiece of Ptolemy of Alexandria (fl. ca. A.D. 140), *Almagest*, was made available to the Moslem reader and as the title indicates it has survived in its Arabic version. Another influential translation was Euclid's *Elements of Geometry*, one of the best-selling books of all time. No parallel experience did the Arab world have until the nineteenth century when the source of translation was Western European rather than Hellenistic.

This period of translation, lasting roughly a century and ending in 850, was followed by one of origination — that is, formulating original thought — which centered in Baghdad and spanned two centuries. Theology and jurisprudence, philology and linguistics, philosophy, medicine, and natural science were the fields that yielded new thoughts. It was a period unparalleled in the whole history of the Arab world. More than that, it can be safely said that in mathematics, astronomy, and medicine, Baghdad scholars of the ninth and tenth centuries had no peers in Europe or Asia. They made of their city a scientific capital of the world, parallel to Athens as the philosophic capital, Rome the legal capital, and Jerusalem the religious capital. Those scholars were of Persian, Turkish, Syrian, Egyptian, Arabian, and other origins, but all wrote in Arabic. They created a largely original, richly endowed civilization and gave Islam its golden age. The entire atmosphere was radically different from that of the Umayyad caliphate.

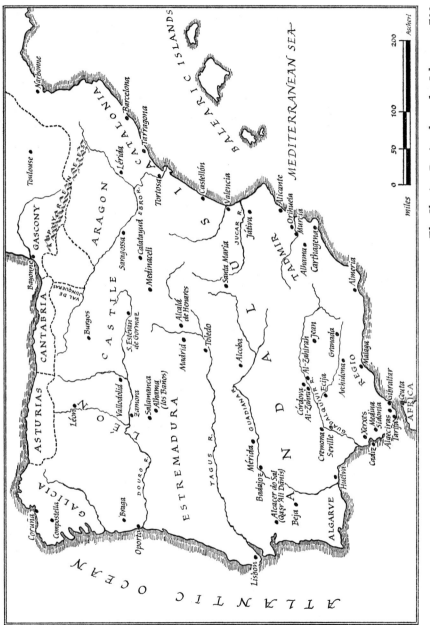

The Iberian Peninsula under Islam, ca. 700

IN MORE than one respect the Umayyad differed from the 'Abbasid caliphate. Under the leadership of the Damascus caliphate wars of conquest were fought; the posture of the Baghdad caliphate was on the whole defensive. The Mediterranean fleet gradually fell into disuse. Only twice was the holy war resumed against the Christian enemy. Both expeditions were under the nominal leadership of young Harun when he was still a crown prince. In the second one (782) the 'Abbasid army for the first and last time reached the Byzantine capital. It was on this occasion that the caliph, father of Harun, bestowed on him the honorific title of *al-Rashid* ("the right-path follower"). Never after did a hostile Arab army threaten the city on the Bosporus.

The Umayyad caliphate was coterminous with Islam; its successor was not. Six years after its establishment the 'Abbasid empire lost its first province, Spain. There in 756 a young Umayyad prince, 'Abd-al-Rahman, who had escaped the slaughter of the Jaffa banquet, inaugurated an independent regime. 'Abd-al-Rahman made Cordova his capital and contented himself with the title of *amir*. This was the first Arab state on European soil. It drew its inspiration from its Damascus ancestor and carried on the Umayyad tradition of tolerance.

The amirate founded by 'Abd-al-Rahman I (756–88) became a caliphate under his namesake and seventh successor, 'Abd-al-Rahman III (912–61). In 929 this 'Abd-al-Rahman, confident of his mounting strength vis-à-vis Baghdad's growing weakness, declared himself caliph. Twenty years earlier a Shi'ite in North Africa, 'Ubaydullah al-Mahdi, had ventured to challenge the 'Abbasids and take the same step. Thus was the world of Islam treated for the first time to the spectacle of three rival headships — two orthodox and one dissident.

Under 'Abd-al-Rahman III and his son al-Hakam (961–76) the Umayyad caliphate in Spain reached its meridian. The realm was extended northward at the expense of the few remaining Christian kinglets and southward to include Morocco and western Algeria. Its trade, industry, and agriculture reached a point of affluence that aroused the admiration if not the envy of contemporary Europe. In pomp and splendor the seat at Cordova vied with Baghdad and Constantinople. It boasted seven hundred mosques — several of which served as schools too — three hundred public baths, a university, and a library. Conspicuous among the places of worship was the congregational mosque begun by 'Abd-al-Rahman I as a rival to the two great sanctuaries in Mecca and Jerusalem. It was enlarged by his successors and completed and beautified by the tenth century. It took its place as the Kaabah of Western Islam. Transformed at the reconquest into a Christian cathedral, it has survived to the present, with its forest of columns and, under the name "La Mezquita," constitutes a chief attraction for tourists.

Equally conspicuous was the imperial palace (al-Zahra') on the slopes of the Sierra overlooking the Guadalquivir outside Cordova. Begun by the new caliph in 936 it took ten thousand men working twenty-five years to complete. It had four hundred rooms and apartments and housed thousands of slaves, guards, and functionaries. A whole city grew around it. Its 4300 columns were imported from Africa and the land of the Franks. Its salon had walls of multicolored marble ornamented with gold. The door had gilded arches of ebony and ivory set with jewels. A nearby convent (San Geronimo) was built with material from its ruins. A heap of refuse in what is called today Old Cordova designates what was once the most sumptuous royal palace in Western Europe.

The other historic monument of Spanish Moslem architecture, Alhambra (al-hamra', "the red one") of Granada, has happily survived almost intact. Granada was the last foothold of Islam in Spain and was lost to Christianity in 1492, an easy date for Americans to remember.

The halo that surrounded the first caliph's court shone even more brilliantly under the second. Indeed the fifteen-year reign of al-Hakam, beginning in 961, was the most peaceful and fruitful one in Moslem Cordova. The caliph was himself a scholar, perhaps unequaled among the caliphs, and he patronized scholars. Thanks to his interest the school founded by his predecessor in the principal mosque became preeminent among European institutions. Preceding the Azhar of Cairo and the Nizamiyah of Baghdad it drew students from the Moslem East as well as the Christian West. To teach these students, professors, especially from Iraq, were invited to occupy distinguished

95

chairs. Next to the university stood the library to which books poured from the intellectual centers of the East. Its forty-four-volume catalog bore four hundred thousand titles. The bibliophile caliph used some of the contents himself, as is indicated by marginal notes in his handwriting. Al-Hakam is also credited with building twenty-seven free schools in provincial capitals.

The Umayyad caliphate in distant al-Andalus (Andalusia) posed less of a threat to 'Abbasid Baghdad than the Fatimid caliphate — which arose in North Africa — especially after the Fatimid seat was removed to Cairo (973). This was done under 'Ubaydullah al-Mahdi's great-grandson al-Mu'izz, conqueror of Egypt. For his capital al-Mu-'izz founded a new city near the old Fustat and named it al-Qahirah (from which Cairo came to English, meaning "ascendant"). In it he built al-Azhar Mosque, the seat of the oldest university extant.

Under al-Mu'izz's son al-'Aziz (975–97) the Fatimid empire reached the apogee of its might and opulence. Its fleet controlled the eastern Mediterranean; its trade with the Italian cities and with Syria, Arabia, and India flourished as never before. Al-'Aziz's name was cited in the Friday sermons from Algeria to Sudan and Yaman and northward to Aleppo in Syria and Mosul (al-Mawsil) in Iraq. So confident was this caliph of victory over his rival in Baghdad that he invested two million dinars in a residence for his future prisoners.

Al-'Aziz's son al-Hakim (996–1021) became the center of a cult named Druzism (after its propagandist al-Darazi) represented today by thousands of adherents in Lebanon and Syria. The decline of the caliphate after his reign was precipitous. It ended in 1171, when the Sunnite Salah-al-Din (Saladin) destroyed the schismatic caliphate and restored the 'Abbasid caliph's name to the Friday congregational prayer.

IV

WHILE the Spanish Umayyad empire was in the making and before the Fatimids began carving their North African empire, minor states east and west were being amputated from the 'Abbasid domain. The pattern was everywhere about the same. Beginning in the ninth century, when the caliph appointed a governor to a distant province, the governor would first remit taxes, inscribe the caliphal name on the local coinage, and mention the caliph's name in the Friday sermons. Gradually, however, he would forget all this, title himself "amir" or "sultan," and pass on the state to his progeny. He might even expand it at the expense of a weak neighbor. Thus, before the end of the tenth century the entire realm from central India to eastern Iraq and from the Oxus to the Persian Gulf had slipped into the hands of various Persian governors. From Persian rule it passed into Turkish hands.

As the wings of the Arab eagle were being clipped, a Perso-Turkish dagger was pointed at its very heart. The exposure to danger began when al-Mu'tasim (833–43), brother of al-Ma'mun, created a bodyguard of Turkish slaves and mercenaries. The corps soon numbered four thousand. Uncultured and arrogant, these Neo-Moslem soldiers made themselves so disagreeable to the Baghdadis that the caliph had to transfer his residence to Samarra, sixty miles north on the Tigris. Through soldiery the former slaves, like the Ottoman Janissaries after them, became the masters. Their commander made and deposed caliphs as the head of the Praetorian guard before him had made and deposed caesars.

An even darker chapter in the life of the 'Abbasid caliphate opened on a December day in 945 when a man who claimed to be a descendant of Chosroes, ibn-Buwayh, appeared at the gates of Baghdad at the head of a horde of followers. The Turkish guard fled. The helpless caliph bestowed upon the new victor, in addition to the title of "amir of amirs" formerly held by the guard's commander, a more honorific one, *Mu'izz-al-Dawlah* ("strengthener of the state"). Hitherto the puppet of a Turkish officer, the head of Islam now became the puppet of a Persian officer, the only difference being that the new master was a Shi'ite. A few weeks after his assumption of power, Mu'izz blinded the caliph, deposed him, and installed a successor. He had his own name stamped on the coinage and mentioned after the caliph's in the weekly sermon.

The Buwayhid dynasty, inaugurated by Mu'izz, endured for more than a century (945–1055). It was in an anomalous position throughout that time. Religiously bound to consider the 'Abbasid caliphate illegitimate, worthy only of destruction, the Buwayhids nevertheless kept the incumbent on the throne to give legitimacy to their own regime. They realized that the ministry they represented was too weak to stand by itself. For all intents and purposes, however, they ruled the empire independently, parceling it out among different members of their family. Following the example of the founder, the dynasts assumed such pompous titles as "the prop of the state," or "the pillar of the state," by which they became known in history. They kept their seats in Persia, leaving Baghdad under a military governor. Their Baghdad palace was called "the abode of the kingdom" and in it they ruled as kings (sing. *malik*, as the old Persian rulers were called). Although these dynasts tried to ingratiate themselves with the populace by avoiding an alliance with the Fatimids of Egypt, by patronizing Arabic literature no less than the Persian, and by other means, they failed. Sunnite resentment and dynastic squabbles finally undermined the authority of the regime and opened the way for a new master.

In addition to the Fatimids and Buwayhids, the third party to play a leading role in the political drama — rather, tragedy — of 'Abbasid Islam was the Saljuq Turks. Named after their chieftain, this Turkish-speaking tribe of nomads in the first half of the eleventh century swept from central Asia into Transoxiana and Persia and from there into western Asia as far as the Bosporous. Somewhere en route they adopted Islam in its Sunnite form. Warlike, tough, and uncultured, they let nothing stand in their way. The collection of petty Turkish and Buwayhid states tumbled before them like a house of cards.

A memorable day in Saljuq history was December 18, 1055, when a grandson of Saljuq, Tughril Beg, was received by the Baghdad caliph as a deliverer, given the title of "sultan" ("he with authority"), and in a ceremonial audience addressed as "king of the east and of the west." Tughril's name was then cited after the caliph's in the Friday prayers.

Tughril's immediate successors became in fact, as in name, kings of the east and of the west. In 1071 the decisive battle of Manzikart (in Armenia), in which the Byzantine emperor Romanus Diogenus was taken prisoner, gave Islam its first firm foothold in the "land of the Romans." It laid the basis of the Turkish domination of Asia Minor. It was the threat posed by these Moslems that prompted the appeal for

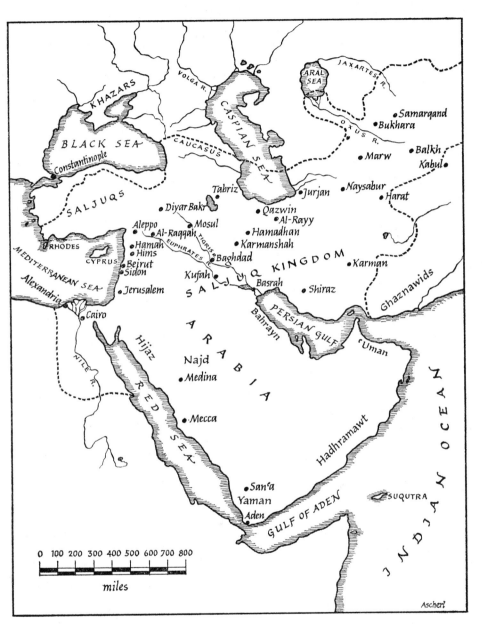

The Caliphal State under the Saljuks, ca. 1100

the First Crusade, and it was they whom the Crusaders encountered in Asia Minor and north Syria.

The Saljuqs served as precursors of their cousins the Ottomans, conquerors of Constantinople and the Balkans. They bequeathed the title of sultan to their followers. Under the Saljuqs the realm of Islam was again united from central through western Asia to near Constantinople and to the border of Egypt. In the tradition of the old Moslems the new conquerors established mosques, schools, libraries, and other pious foundations. One of their viziers, Nizam-al-Mulk, a Persian and an ornament in the political history of Islam, established (1065) the schools named after him and emulated by other schools throughout the realm. The Saljuqs provide another example of barbarian infidels fastening the yoke over the necks of Moslems, embracing their religion, and then becoming the staunch champions of the new religion and the new culture.

Saljuq domination in Baghdad lasted for more than a century and a third (1055–1194). It was challenged by al-Nasir (1180–1225), the first able 'Abbasid caliph in centuries — and the last one. (For almost three centuries al-Nasir's predecessors reigned but did not rule.) But this caliph's attempt to restore the office to something of its former power was not entirely successful. The Turkish shah of Khwarizm, whose aid he sought in destroying the Saljuqs, came as a friend and — as often happens in history — remained as an enemy. In the meantime a new and more formidable enemy for both was looming on the eastern horizon: Chingiz Khan, invincible warrior and founder of the world's largest empire.

v

RIDING fleet horses, armed with strange bows, and pushed by some unknown force, these wild Mongols (identified as Tatars in Arabic sources) constituted the greatest migratory wave in a series of invasions that had begun earlier and continued into later centuries. Startling in the rapidity of its execution, this campaign of Chingiz Khan was far-reaching in its results. To the Arab chroniclers of the day the horde looked as if it comprised seven hundred thousand men, although even including recruits it could not have been at any time

100

more than a fourth of that number. Like a cyclone, the warriors swept from their habitat through the steppes of Asia into the world of Islam, leaving a crimson stream bordered with heaps of ruin in their trail. One after the other of the Moslem cities of Transoxiana and Khurasan, brilliant centers of Islamic civilization, were devastated. Bukhara was utterly destroyed by fire (1220), but its mosques were spared to serve as stables for the conquerors' horses. Samarqand, seeking to escape the same fate, surrendered, but that did not save it from plunder and its people from slaughter or deportation. For a century and a half the city survived as a shadow of its former self. In the following year Balkh (Gr. Baktra) was ruined and never recovered. Harat (in Afghanistan) was twice devastated, but it recovered. According to Arab estimates, in Marw, former capital of Khurasan, seven hundred thousand men, women, and children were slaughtered. Even if allowance is made for refugees from the neighborhood the estimates remain too high. The oasis that was Marw was then converted into a desert. In Naysabur, where a Mongol general was killed, orders were issued to destroy the city so that its site would be plowable. The only survivors were four hundred artisans who were sent to Mongolia. Even the dogs and cats were not spared. The celebrated historian ibn-al-Athir (born in Mosul, 1234) shuddered at the narration of these horrors and wished his mother had not borne him.

Baghdadis lived in daily terror of being next, but the course of the army took another direction. It bypassed the shuddering capital of Islam. Crossing the Caucasus it overran Georgia, southern Russia, Crimea, and Bulgaria. There the empire founded by the chief of a petty Mogul tribe reached its limit, stretching from the China Sea almost to the shores of the Adriatic.

Baghdad, however, was not spared for long. The city bypassed by Chingiz was aimed at by his grandson Hulagu. Leading the next westward migratory movement, this Mongol in 1265 destroyed the Persian strongholds of the Assassin order, headed by their "mother convent" of Alamut, and in the following year addressed an ultimatum to the caliph demanding unconditional surrender. Al-Musta'sim's reply was evasive. In January 1258 siege was laid to the city and Mongol mangonels had no difficulty in effecting a breach in its walls. Hulagu refused to receive a delegation headed by the vizir accompanied by the Nestorian catholicos (the invader had a Christian wife). The city was stormed and plundered. Its people, including the caliphal family and officials, were indiscriminately put to the sword. The reported eight hundred thousand victims were perhaps a tenth that many, including refugees. So offensive were the odors from the corpses strewn in the streets that even the terrible Mongols had to keep away for several days. Al-Musta'sim (1242–58) was the thirty-seventh 'Abbasid caliph and the last. This was the first time in the history of Islam that Friday prayers were conducted with no mention of a caliph's name.

VI

WITH al-Musta'sim the Arab state can be said to have come to an end — never to rise again. Its failure was partly due to its inability to integrate its varied ethnic elements within its structure. A rash of successor states, mostly Mongol, Turkish, and Persian, erupted all over the surface of the land. Prominent among them was the Mamluk of Egypt-Syria-Hijaz. The Mamluks ("possessed"), as their name indicates, were a dynasty of slaves, mostly Turkish and Circasian, who for over two and a half centuries ruled the mainland of the Arabs as a military oligarchy. In 1261 one of their distinguished sultans, Baybars, harbored a fugitive uncle of the last caliph and set him up as a puppet caliph to bolster the alien Mamluk regime. When the Ottoman sultan Salim destroyed the Mamluk state in 1517 he took among his prisoners a nonentity, titled *al-Mutawakkil*, who claimed to be in the 'Abbasid line. The claim that al-Mutawakkil passed on the caliphate to Salim's successors is not substantiated. The Ottomans, however, assumed the caliphal title, although they were not only non-Qurayshites, but non-Arabs as well.

The Ottoman caliphate was abolished in 1924 by the Turkish reformer Mustafa Kemal. All attempts since then to revive the Arab caliphal state have ended in failure. Most notable among the attempts was that of the Sharif ("descendant of the Prophet") of Mecca and king of Hijaz, Husayn, whose proclamation (1916) of succession to the defunct caliphate evoked little response in the Moslem world. Husayn's descendants ruled for a time over Iraq and they still rule in Jordan, but any similarity between the modern Arab states and the caliphal one is purely superficial.

Even before the destruction of the Arab caliphate not only the political but the cultural streams of life were beginning to flow in other than Arab channels. This transition will be made clear in the following chapters.

الجزء الثالث : الاسلام كثقافة

PART III *Islam the Culture*

ARAB SCIENCE

✦ISLAM the culture, as was pointed out in the first chapter, unlike Islam the religion and Islam the state, was preponderantly the product of the intellectual activity of conquered peoples Arabicized and Islamized. A highly synthetic compound of disparate elements, it was interracial and interreligious. Moslems, Christians, and Jews, Semites, Hamites, and Indo-Europeans, all participated in its production. What is then called Arab culture or Moslem civilization was Arab in the sense of its being expressed in the Arabic language, rather than being the product of Arabians, and it was Moslem in the sense of its having been developed during the Moslem era and to an extent under caliphal auspices.

Language, next to religion, constituted the major enduring contribution of Arabians. For some three hundred years, beginning in the mid-eighth century, Arabic was the vehicle for transmitting scientific, philosophic, and literary thought, which was quantitatively and qualitatively superior to anything being transmitted in Latin, Hindi, Chinese, or any other language.

Of the three Islams, Islam the culture was the last to achieve ascendancy. Outside Arabia proper, Islam the state was first. Next, Islam the religion gained ground. Conquered peoples — even privileged dhimmis — were slow to appreciate the political and economic advantages of professing the new religion. As they were Islamized they became Arabicized, since Arabic was the official private language as well as the formal prayer language. Iraq and Egypt were the first to succumb to Islam the religion. Mount Lebanon proved an effective barrier to the religion and language of Arabia, and so Lebanon never came within Islam's fold completely. Certain villages there maintained their native Syriac tongue until the sixteenth century. Nevertheless, the path lay open for the rise and spread of Islamic culture, even in mountainous Lebanon.

The Arabic word for science ('ilm), like its English correspondent, etymologically means "knowledge," or "learning." It may be used in a broad sense to mean knowledge systematized with reference to general truths and laws, or more specifically, to refer to knowledge as it relates to the physical world, in which case it is known as physical or natural science.

In science, using the term in its restricted sense, the Arabians had no previous knowledge on which to build. Their pre-Islamic culture, being largely illiterate, could not have developed physical or natural science, nor could it have had much abstract science such as mathematics and astronomy. Whatever knowledge the early Arabians possessed of the stars, mathematics, and treatment of diseases — the three scientific fields in which the Arabs later excelled — must have been transmitted orally through folklore.

Arabian interest in these three areas was prompted by utilitarian considerations. Calculation was a necessity for urban populations living on trade, as in Mecca. Celestial phenomena, striking and easy to observe, must have aroused the wonder of even primitive man. Arabian heathenism featured astral beliefs. The Bedouins worshiped the moon, for if the heat of the day made grazing prohibitive the moon provided light by which the nomads could graze their flocks. In his agricultural stage the Arabian began to emphasize sun worship. As Semites the early Arabians shared the same astrological beliefs with their neighbors to the north, but they developed no elaborate mythology, no involved theology, and no cosmogony comparable to those of the Babylonians.

Interest in plants and animals was prompted by the need for food and ultimately led to the study of biology, which in turn prompted the study of medicine. Medical lore in early Arabia, as in other primitive cultures, was so hopelessly intermingled with magic and superstition that it could make no progress. Early Arabic literature has preserved references to the use of herbs and seeds as remedies. It also mentions the so-called Prophetic medicine, emphasizing the use of honey. The abuse of this form of medicine may be illustrated by the story of the practitioner who once prescribed honey for a Bedouin's stomach ailment, and when the patient's brother reported the ineffectiveness of the remedy, the practitioner replied, "Allah's Prophet is truthful; but your brother's belly is false."

Only after they had been exposed to the influence of Islam and of other cultures did the Arabians become aware of the existing body of scientific knowledge. It was the Moslem conquests of the early century that established vital contact between them and the rich cultural tradition represented by Greeks, Syrians, Persians, and Egyptians. In medicine and other sciences, in philosophy, and in art and architecture the sons of the desert had little to teach and much to learn. It is to their credit, however, that they appreciated that fact and encouraged their subjects to preserve and promote their local traditions so long as they did not conflict with Islam. Throughout the caliphal period the bearers of the torch of learning were first Christians and then new converts from Persia, Syria, and other conquered territories.

I

THE period of translation, discussed in the preceding chapter, was followed by a period of origination lasting in the East for some two centuries. The two periods overlap, since some translators were themselves originators. Hunayn ibn-Ishaq, dean of Christian translators, wrote a book on eye diseases which has been published in English translation as the earliest extant text on ophthalmology. For the Arabs those two centuries of scientific activity centered in Baghdad constitute the golden age, corresponding to the fifth and fourth pre-Christian centuries in Athens.

The galaxy of scholars in the scientific firmament of Islam was ushered in by a Baghdadi of Persian origin. His specialty was mathematics and astronomy. His name, al-Khwarizmi (Muhammad ibn-Musa), gave us the words "algorism" and "algorithm" (from Lat. *algorismus*), meaning "arithmetic" or "the science of calculating by means of nine figures and zero." Besides his last name, his Arabic designation "al-Majusi" (Zoroastrian, Magian) leaves no doubt of his non-Arab, non-Moslem origin. Al-Khwarizmi's earliest biographer, fellow Baghdadi al-Nadim, mentions in his *Fihrist* neither the date or place of his birth, nor the date or place of his death. All that is known is that he flourished between 813 and 846, partly while a resident of al-Ma'mun's House of Wisdom, one of the rare places in Islam with facilities for creative work. Strangely al-Nadim cites as books written by his subject those on the astrolabe, sundial, and history — all lost — but fails to mention the books on arithmetic and algebra, to which al-Khwarizmi largely owed his international fame.

Al-Khwarizmi's contribution to astronomy was the construction of astronomical tables (*zij*), which were based on Indian sources. Revised almost a century and a half later by the Moslem Spanish astronomer al-Majriti and translated (1126) into Latin by the English scholar Adelard of Bath, al-Khwarizmi's tables became the basis for other works in the East and West. In due course they replaced their Greek and Indian predecessors and were used by scholars as far away as China. In his translation al-Majriti used the word *jayb* ("pocket") which was translated into Latin as *sinus*, from which comes the English "sine."

Another contribution by al-Khwarizmi was an atlas (Ar. *surah*, "image") of the heavens and the earth, compiled in collaboration with sixty-nine others at the request of their patron al-Ma'mun. It was the first in Arabic. In the preparation of this work the author used Ptolemy's geography, which he had revised and enlarged. The caliph's astronomers (whether al-Khwarizmi was one of them is not certain) performed in the Syrian desert a most delicate geodetic operation — the measuring of a terrestrial degree. Their aim was to determine the size of the earth and its circumference, based on the assumption that the earth was round. The measurement yielded 56⅔ Arabic miles, exceeding the exact length by only 2877 feet.

Al-Ma'mun is credited with constructing the first observatory in

Islam. Others were built in Persia, Syria, and Egypt. The instruments — among them the astrolabe, quadrant, and armillary globe representing the celestial sphere — must have been primitive. The caliph's astrologer Ibrahim al-Fazari was reportedly the first to manufacture an Arab astrolabe.

Unlike later Arab scientists and philosophers, the mathematician and astronomer al-Khwarizmi depended more on Hindi than on Greek sources, since the translations from the latter were still in their infancy. Specifically his source was the mathematical and astronomical material brought by a Hindu roving scholar (771) to the court of al-Mansur and translated by al-Fazari into Arabic under the title *Sindhind* (Hindi *Siddhanta*).

Al-Khwarizmi's work on arithmetic, evidently the oldest in Arabic — at least the oldest to use what the Arabs call Hindi numerals and the Europeans call Arabic numerals — has survived in its Latin translation. The original title must have meant "the book on addition and subtraction Hindi style." It introduced the numerical system — evolved if not devised by Indians — into both the East and West. Included with the numerals was the zero or cipher (from Ar. *sifr* ["empty"]), which was probably an Arab invention. Two early Latin works on arithmetic, *Carmen de Algorismo* (by Alexander de Villa Dei, ca. 1220) and *Algorismus vulgaris* (by John of Halifax, ca. 1250), bear the Arab arithmetician's name.

Not only was al-Khwarizmi a father of arithmetic, but he was the originator of algebra, too. His *Hisab al-Jabr w-al-Muqabalah* ("the calculation of integration and equation") isolated, systematized, and transmitted this science to Moslems and Christians. The Arabic original survived in a unique manuscript written about five centuries after the author's death and preserved in the library of Oxford University. In it the numerical system was also used. In Latin *algorismus* came also to mean the Arabic numerals; Chaucer in his *Treatise on the Astrolabe* corrupts it further into "augrim" or "augrym."

Translated into Latin first by Robert of Chester (ca. 1145) and then by the dean of translators in the Toledo school, Gerard of Cremona (Italy, d. 1187), al-Khwarizmi's *al-Jabr* soon established itself as the standard work in its field. In the introduction to it the author mod-

110

estly states that the book was written with the encouragement of al-Ma'mun, who suggested a short, simplified work that people could use in their everyday dealings as well as in calculating their inheritances and surveying their lands. How much the author owed to Indian and Babylonian (through Syriac) sources, modern research has not been able to ascertain. Among medieval mathematicians influenced by this work mention should be made of Leonardo Fibonacci of Pisa (d. after 1240), who traveled in the Near East; Master Jacob of Florence, whose Italian treatise on mathematics (1307) contains the six types of quadratic equations given by the Arab algebraist; and 'Umar al-Khayyam (d. 1123), more celebrated in the West for his Persian love poems than for his astronomical and mathematical contributions.

Europeans were slow to appreciate the Arab gift of numerals. The new system, it was argued, lent itself more readily to falsification, especially in keeping accounts. It was not until the sixteenth century that a general realization of the wide mathematical horizons opened up by the new device was achieved. It was the use of these numerals that made modern progress in mathematical science possible. As for the zero, the function it performs is unique. It enables us to keep the proper ranks in the series of powers (tens, hundreds, etc.) when one of those powers is not represented. Twenty-two becomes two hundred and two or two thousand and two by the simple device of interposing one or two zeros, whereas a radical change would be necessary if Roman numerals were used.

Successors of al-Khwarizmi in Baghdad — al-Raqqah (Syria) and al-Rayy and Naysabur (Persia) — continued their systematic studies of the heavens and further enriched man's knowledge of mathematics. One successor was al-Battani (abu-'Abdullah Muhammad, d. 929), of Harran Sabian origin, who carried on his observations at al-Raqqah. Following al-Khwarizmi, al-Battani compiled astronomical tables and made important emendations to Ptolemy's theories. One of the Ptolemaic doctrines he exploded was the immobility of the solar apogee. Al-Battani's tables, embodying his observations, were translated twice into Latin in the twelfth century and once into Spanish in the thirteenth century. Published repeatedly in the sixteenth and seventeenth centuries, they made the Latin equivalent of his name, Albategnius, familiar in learned circles. The effect of his tables on the development of astronomical science and spherical trigonometry was noticeable in later Arabic and Latin works. With al-Battani mathematics became increasingly subservient to astronomy. His observations of solar and lunar eclipses remained in vogue in Europe until the mid-eighteenth century.

This Syrian Moslem scholar rectified the calculations of the orbit of the moon, determined with greater accuracy the obliquity of the ecliptic, and proved the possibility of annular eclipses of the sun. The fact that he was able to accomplish what he did, considering the conditions under which he worked, adds luster to his name.

II

AS ARAB science decayed in the Eastern soil of Islam, it flourished in its Western soil. There Cordova took the place of Baghdad as the center of learning, while Toledo and Seville shared in the intellectual effort. Spanish Arab scholars built on foundations laid by their coreligionists in Iraq, Syria, Egypt, and Persia. Their golden prime covered roughly the eleventh and twelfth centuries.

One of the first scholars of this era was the mathematician-astronomer Maslamah al-Majriti. Al-Majriti was born in Madrid — as his name indicates — but flourished in Cordova, where he died about 1007. He traveled in the East and made a special study of the works of his Eastern predecessors. Among other contributions he converted the basis of al-Khwarizmi's tables from the Persian to the Moslem era, thereby determining the approximate position of the planets at the time of the hijrah.

He also turned his attention to the problem of locating the meridian of the world. Early Arab geographers had picked up from Indian sources the theory that there was a world center — perhaps a cupola or summit — lying an equal distance from the four cardinal points. This they called *arin*, from the name of the Indian town that was at one time the supposed world center. The arin doctrine finally found its way into a Latin work (1410) from which, it is believed, Christopher Columbus adopted the notion that the earth was pear-shaped and had in its Western hemisphere, opposite the Indian arin, a corresponding elevated center. An Arab doctrine may then be claimed to have had a share in the greatest geographic discovery of modern times.

The so-called Toledan tables were based on studies and observations conducted by Hispano-Arab scholars, notable among whom was al-Zarqali (abu-Ishaq Ibrahim, d. ca. 1087). The tables, of course, included material derived from Eastern Arab sources. Rendered into Latin by Gerard of Cremona, they served as a main source for French and other European works. Al-Zarqali was the first to prove the motion of the solar apogee with reference to the stars. His mathematical contributions included explanation of the trigonometrical tables.

In his masterpiece Copernicus, regarded as the founder of modern astronomy and father of the theory that the earth rotates on its axis and that the planets revolve in orbits around the sun, mentions both al-Battani (Albategnius) and al-Zarqali (Arzachel).

III

IN TWO fields allied to astronomy — astrology and geography — Arab scholars made noteworthy advances. Most of the astronomers mentioned above were also astrologers to the caliphs or sultans under whose rule they lived. To modern minds astrology, based on the assumption that astral influence determines man's fate, is a pseudo-science, but not to the ancients or to medieval Christians and Moslems. Astrology stands in the same relation to astronomy that alchemy stands in relation to chemistry, and witchcraft to medicine. Not only rulers consulted astrologers before undertaking an enterprise but ordinary men and women, too, sought their guidance for the future. 'Abd-al-'Aziz, the founder of the modern Su'udi (Saudi) dynasty, had his astrologer, as al-Ma'mun had his.

The most distinguished figure in Arab astrology was a Khurasani resident of Baghdad, abu-Ma'shar (Ja'far ibn-Muhammad, d. 886). Abu-Ma'shar utilized his predecessors' works, plagiarized two works by his contemporary, the celebrated philosopher al-Kindi, and disseminated the material east and west. His principal writings were rendered in the twelfth century into Latin by John of Seville and Adelard of Bath and became the most frequently quoted by medieval authors. Aspects of astronomical geography relating to the causation of tides reached the West through those translations.

The Moslem abu-Ma'shar, metamorphosed into Latin as Albumasar, was accepted as a prophet by medieval Christians, and worked his way into Christian iconography.

The obligation of holy pilgrimage and the need for determining the proper direction for prayer gave religious impulse to the study of geography. Astrology, necessary for determining the latitudes and longitudes of places, added to its influence. Arab traders and navigators, who between the eighth and tenth centuries roamed over a large part of the then-known world, brought back reports that aroused interest and added to the body of geographic knowledge. Several scholars undertook journeys themselves in quest of further geographical facts, with the result that from the ninth to the fourteenth century the richest geographic output was in Arabic. Al-Biruni (abu-al-Bayhan Ahmad, d. 1050), a native of Afghanistan, visited India and wrote a classic description of it. He observed that the Indus valley must have been an ancient sea that had been filled up with alluvium. Among his scientific contributions was an explanation of the working of natural springs by the hydrostatic principle.

Much of the geographical material gradually worked its way into the monumental six-volume *Mu'jam al-Buldan* ("geographical dictionary") which was compiled in 1228 by a former Greek slave, Yaqut (al-Rumi, "the Roman"). The book, alphabetically arranged, is a veritable encyclopedia containing — in addition to geographical facts — historical, ethnographic, and scientific data.

But the outstanding geographer and cartographer in the Arab — if not in the medieval — world was of Hispano-Arab parentage and Moroccan nativity, abu-'Abdullah Muhammad al-Idrisi (d. 1166). Al-Idrisi lived at the court of Roger II, the Norman king of Sicily. The island was then the meeting place of two cultural areas. Like al-Ma'-mun, Roger asked his protégé to prepare a comprehensive geography and construct a world map. In the introduction of his book *Kitab Rujar* ("the Rogerian treatise") al-Idrisi states that he incorporated original material acquired by observers sent to various lands. He, moreover, showed originality in collating the material and in recogniz-

114

ing the fact of the earth's sphericity. His map of the world places the sources of the Nile, supposedly a nineteenth-century discovery, approximately where they should be.

Regrettably literary Arabic geography claimed no attention on the part of Latin translators and therefore left no impression on European thought. Other than the astronomical geography referred to above, no traces are noticeable in Western literature. Even al-Idrisi was overlooked. The first known Latin rendition of his work was done in Rome (1619) by two Maronite scholars in an abridged form and without acknowledging the author's name.

IV

ARAB contributions to medicine were no less significant or enduring than those to mathematics or astronomy. Arab knowledge of scientific medicine probably began in al-Ma'mun's time when the Christian Hunayn ibn-Ishaq translated Galen. For centuries Galen's works became as authoritative in Arab medical practice as they were earlier in Roman and Greek practice. Galen in Arabic provided the Moslem practitioner with the first opportunity to become "modernized." By the end of the ninth century the Christian monopoly on the field was broken, passing before long into the hands of Moslems, mostly Persians, who wrote, of course, in Arabic.

The series of distinguished Moslem physicians is headed by al-Razi (Nuh ibn-Zakariya, 865–925), whose last name is derived from his birthplace al-Rayy outside the modern capital of Persia. Al-Razi began his career studying alchemy under Hunayn and ended it as a physician and surgeon. Like his predecessor al-Kindi and his successor ibn-Sina he was also a philosopher but, unlike them, he made no attempt to reconcile Greek philosophy and Islamic religion. To him the two were irreconcilable. In fact he was a radical thinker, a rationalist who rejected the concept of prophecy, challenged koranic dogma, and subordinated theology to philosophy. In this respect he was rare if not exceptional in Islam.

In medicine as in philosophy this physician was original. He was one of the first to exercise a measure of empirical spirit and reject oc-

115

cultist explanations. In surgery he was one of the first to use the seton. His method of choosing a site for a new hospital building in Baghdad — by hanging up shreds of meat in different places of the city to determine the degree of putrefaction — indicates originality in thinking. Of the two hundred works ascribed to al-Razi — half of which have been lost — thirteen are about alchemy. Two of his medical works may be singled out: *al-Hawi* ("the comprehensive book") and *al-Judari w-al-Hasbah* ("smallpox and measles").

True to its name *al-Hawi* was a veritable medical encyclopedia summing up what the Arabs knew of Greek, Syriac, Persian, and Hindi medicine and enriched by the addition of the author's experiments and experiences. The author spent fifteen years compiling it and used probably more words than ibn-Sina in *al-Qanun*. A publisher in Hydarabad has already issued eighteen volumes of it (1955–65) and promises more. The book was first translated into Latin (1279) under the auspices of Charles, king of Naples and Sicily, by the Jewish physician Faraj ben-Salim, translator of other Arabic medical works. Under the title *Continens* it soon established itself as a standard text and was repeatedly printed from 1486 onward. A fifth edition appeared in Venice in 1542. The invention of printing from movable type in the mid-fifteenth century facilitated the distribution of al-Razi's and other Arab scholars' works. It made the name Rhazes familiar in medical schools.

Al-Razi's monograph on smallpox and measles, an ornament of Arab medical literature, is considered the earliest of its kind. In it the author gave the first clinical account of smallpox and distinguished it from measles. Translated into Latin, it was printed about forty times between 1498 and 1866; it was translated into a number of modern languages including English (1848). It confirmed the author's reputation as one of the keenest thinkers and greatest clinicians not only of Islam but of Christendom.

It was not long before *al-Hawi* had a competitor in *al-Kitab al-Maliki* ("the royal book," *Liber regius*) by 'Ali al-'Abbas (Haly Abbas) al-Majusi (d. 994). The book was dedicated to the author's patron, a Buwayhid sultan. Like its predecessor it was a treasure house of the science and practice of medicine, but this latter work was more concise. It advanced medical knowledge by presenting a number of

116

points, then new, including a rudimentary conception of the capillary system, and evidence that in the act of delivery the baby does not come out by itself but is pushed by the muscular contraction of the womb. A Damascene physician who served as dean of the Mamluk hospital in Cairo, ibn-al-Nafis (d. 1288), added a clear conception of the pulmonary circulation of the blood. That was two and a half centuries before the time of Harvey, the Englishman who is generally credited with the discovery. What makes ibn-al-Nafis' discovery especially remarkable is the fact that it was arrived at by deduction rather than by dissection. The thirteenth-century physician has been described as one "who would not prescribe medicine when diet sufficed."

Earlier than the comprehensive encyclopedia, "the royal book" was translated in part into Latin by Constantine the African (d. 1087) and wholly by the Pisan Stephen of Antioch. It was the only major Arabic work the Crusaders carried back with them to Europe.

The works of al-Razi and al-Majusi were in due course superseded as textbooks and outlived in usage by those of ibn-Sina, titled by his people *al-shaykh al-ra'is* ("the dean of the learned and the chief of courtiers"). The title was well deserved. Ibn-Sina distinguished himself as a physician, philosopher, scientist, and vizir. He is generally considered the greatest physician of the early Middle Ages.

Al-Husayn, to use his first name, was born in 980 near Bukhara (Transoxiana) and wrote primarily in Arabic except for a few works in Persian. When he was sixteen years old, according to his autobiography, he had mastered a number of the then-known sciences, including medicine which he "found easy." He then started on his career as a teacher and a practitioner. The fame of the prodigy reached the ailing Samanid governor of Bukhara, and when the young physician cured him he was granted the privilege of using the well-stocked royal library. In eighteen months he reportedly had devoured the contents of the entire library.

Of the forty-three medical works authored by ibn-Sina his masterpiece was *al-Qanun fi al-Tibb* ("the canon in medicine"), which he completed in the course of a turbulent career at Hamadhan. The book summarized in a million words the Hippocratic and Galenic traditions, synthetized with Syro-Arabic and Indo-Persian sources and supple-

117

mented by the author's experience and experimentation. He made even old material in it look new and usable: more methodical in arrangement, classification, and presentation than *al-Hawi*, *al-Qanun* represented the culmination of Arab systematization of medical science. It established itself as the supreme medical authority in the world of Islam until the nineteenth century. Its success in the West was almost equally spectacular. Translated by Gerard of Cremona, the *Canon* in the last third of the fifteenth century appeared in three Latin editions and one Hebrew edition. Gerard, the Italian counterpart of Hunayn, the Arab translator, is credited with translating no fewer than eighty Arabic works, about three-fourths of the total number of Arabic works translated into Latin. The *Canon* was used as a text in the universities of Paris and Louvain till the mid-seventeenth century. In the words of a modern historian of medicine, it "remained a medical bible for a longer period than any other work."

The book covered general medicine, pathology, and pharmacology, told how to treat diseases affecting all parts of the body from head to foot, recognized the importance of dietetics, the effect of climate on health, and the close relation between emotional and physiological conditions. Alchemy was denounced. Among other features were its discussions of the contagious nature of consumption, and the spreading of disease by soil and water. In surgery it recommended medicated wine as an oral anesthetic.

Surgery was not one of the fields in which Arabs made a distinct contribution. Islam, as interpreted by its ulama, discouraged dissection, a prerequisite for understanding the body's anatomy. It was Western Islam, where traditional ties were loose, that produced the greatest Arab surgeon and one of the greatest of medieval Europe, abu-al-Qasim (Abulcasis) al-Zahrawi (d. ca. 1013).

Al-Zahrawi was the court physician of al-Hakam, under whom the Umayyad caliphate of Cordova enjoyed its heyday. Al-Zahrawi's claim to distinction rests on his *al-Tasrif fi Man 'Ajaz 'an al-Ta'lif* ("an aid to him who lacks ability to use large treatises"). The book included a detailed surgical section, the first of its kind, summarizing the surgical knowledge of the time. This part was translated first into Latin by the indefatigable Gerard and then into Provençal and Hebrew. In the mid-fourteenth century a distinguished French surgeon incorporated that part into his book. It passed through many editions including one in Venice (1497), another in Basel (1541), and a third in Oxford (1778). For centuries al-Zahrawi's book was used as a text in the medical schools of Salerno, Montpellier, and elsewhere. It either introduced or emphasized cauterization of wounds and it described crushing of stones inside the bladder. It also brought out the necessity of dissection and even vivisection. A feature of the book was illustrations of instruments used by the author, instruments which served as models in Asia and Europe.

In two fields related to medicine — alchemy and botany — Arab progress was no less remarkable than in medicine itself. It is enough to merely recall that the word for the medieval chemical science of alchemy was of Arabic origin (*al-kimiya'*), that the father of this "science" was an Eastern Moslem, Jabir ibn-Hayyan (fl. ca. 775), and that the best known herbalist and botanist after Dioscorides was a Western Moslem, ibn-al-Baytar of Malaga (d. 1248).

Alchemy originated in Greek Egypt and reached its peak of popularity in medieval Iraq. By the fourteenth century the treatises of Jabir (Geber), genuine or spurious, had established themselves as the most influential chemical works in Asia and Europe. Moslem alchemists everywhere recognized him as their master. Ibn-al-Baytar's researches covered southern Spain and the littoral of North Africa and Syria and were embodied in his *al-Jami' fi al-Adwiyah al-Mufradah* ("collection of simple remedies") from the vegetable, animal, and mineral worlds. A part of it was published under the title *Simplicia* as late as 1758 at Cremona.

In the course of their fanatical hunt for those two will-o'-the-wisps — the elixir of life and the transmutation of base into precious metal — Arab alchemists developed new techniques in processing metals and made valuable scientific discoveries. They improved on the two principal chemical operations of calcination and reduction, as well as on the methods of evaporation, sublimation, melting, and crystallization. They introduced new chemical elements and substances such as antimony (*ithmid*), arsenic (*zirnikh*), realgar (*rahj al-ghar*), borax

119

(*bawraq*), and alkali (*al-qili*). They were also responsible for introducing implements such as alembics (*al-inbiq*) and aludel (*al-uthal*).

Arab physicians, no less than Arab alchemists, left linguistic traces familiar to all students of medicine. Certain medical terms — alcohol (*al-kuhl*), julep (*julab*), rob (*rubb*), soda (*suda'*), and syrup (*sharab*) — are loanwords. Other words came to English through Latin translations: *dura mater* (*al-umm al-jafiyah*, "coarse mother," the tough membrane enveloping the brain) and *pia mater* (*al-umm al-raqiqah*, "thin mother," the thin membrane covering the brain). Arab astronomers left on the skies traces of their industry discernible to all who read the names of the stars: Acrab (*'aqrab*, "scorpion"), Algedi (*al-jadi*, "the kid"), Altair (*al-ta'ir*, "the flyer"), Deneb (*dheneb*, "tail"), Pherkad (*farqad*, "calf"). They testify to the rich legacy of Islam to Christian Europe.

PHILOSOPHY

✦ IN COMMON with other Semites, the Arabs developed no system that could be called philosophy — unless it was their religious system. They did, however, have philosophy in its etymological sense, "love of wisdom." Their early literature is rich in proverbs, wise sayings, anecdotes, and fables intended to inculcate courage, hospitality, tribal solidarity, and other virtues high in their scale of values. Their respect for the wise man (*hakim*, the same word as is used for physician) was great. The pre-Islamic Arab sage Luqman was adopted by Muhammad as the wise maker of proverbs and subsequently consecrated in the Koran, where a surah (31) bears his name. In Islam the Prophet's cousin and son-in-law 'Ali became the legendary sage to whom, like Solomon, numerous wise sayings have been attributed.

With the Moslem conquest of the Syriac-speaking Christians of the Fertile Crescent, the channel was opened for transmitting not only Greek science but Greek philosophy. These Christians, like the Jews before them, depended on revelation for ascertaining the truth and depended on faith for accepting it. To them the supernatural was not necessarily irrational, and they labored hard to integrate the new exotic elements of Greek philosophy into their theology. For polemical purposes Aristotelian logic was especially useful. The Greeks, on the other hand, trusted reason and, more than any other people of antiquity, made intellect the arbiter in determining what was true.

The philosophy with which the Christians concerned themselves, however, was not of the fourth pre-Christian century of Plato and Aristotle in Athens but of the fourth Christian century in Alexandria; it was known as Neoplatonism. This system synthetized Platonic metaphysical elements and Aristotelian logic with Stoic ethical teachings and Oriental mystical ingredients. One of its founders was born in Tyre and bore the Semitic name Melik ("king"), but became better known by his Latin name, Porphyry ("clad in purple," d. ca. A.D. 305). It was this Neoplatonic philosophy that Syrian Christians transmitted to the Arab Moslems either directly from Greek or through Syriac. Plato became known through his Hellenistic form, not his Hellenic original, and likewise his pupil Aristotle appeared in Neoplatonic garb.

The confrontation between Islam and philosophy in ninth-century Baghdad raised vexatious problems and paradoxes. The new element looked dangerously exotic, difficult if not impossible to accommodate. It was given a non-Arabic name, *falsafah*. Theologians and legists were — predictably — the first to raise their voices against it. Their control over the mass mind amounted to a monopoly. To them accommodation or coexistence entailed the subordination of theology to philosophy — in which case there would be no more theology — or the subordination of philosophy to theology — in which case there was no need for philosophy. The impasse was at last broken by the first Arab philosopher.

I

THE man was — for once — a pure-blooded Arabian (mothers' blood did not count) of the royal tribe of Kindah of Yamani origin. Abu-Yusuf Ya'qub al-Kindi (ca. 801–73) was therefore styled *faylasuf al-'Arab*. He was not only the first formal Arab philosopher but the last in the Eastern caliphate. Born in Kufah, where his father was governor, educated at Basrah, and domiciled in Baghdad, Ya'qub had the opportunity to acquire the finest education that the three leading intellectual centers of Iraq could offer. Besides the traditional koranic and linguistic sciences, the gifted youth studied medicine and delved into Mu'tazilah's writings, which were impregnated with Greek thought. This

122

led him to the study of Aristotle's metaphysics, translated by Hunayn, and to the pseudo-Aristotelian theology, written by an unknown Neoplatonist and translated into Arabic for al-Kindi by a Christian from Hims (Syria). In Baghdad the budding philosopher joined the luminous galaxy of the caliphal court. He soon became the court physician and counselor as well as the tutor to Ahmad, son of al-Mu'tasim, brother and successor (in 833) to al-Ma'mun.

Al-Kindi started his philosophical career by attracting attention immediately. In the first treatise, dedicated to his patron al-Mu'tasim, he defined falsafah as "the knowledge of things as they are in reality," making it a comprehensive system embracing religious, political, physical, mathematical, and other sciences. To him as to others in those days philosophy was the mother of the sciences. To his definition he added that truth as ascertained by philosophy is universal and supreme. It transcends nationality and denomination and should be so accepted even if the source is foreign. He soon found himself in deep trouble. The exponents of orthodoxy rejected his definition as nonsense. He sought refuge in reservations. Prophetic truth, he argued, is spontaneous, requiring no effort. It is acceptable by faith. There is no contradiction between conclusions drawn by faith and those of philosophic sciences arrived at by rational reasoning and intellectual exertion. Al-Kindi thus opened the way to the establishment of a double standard of truth: one for the elites, who are guided by reason, and the other for the masses, who are guided by faith.

Islamic revelation on two major doctrines — resurrection and creation — is specific and diametrically opposed to the Aristotelian views. Neoplatonism taught that resurrection was of the soul only — an outright heresy in Islam, which insists on individual bodily rebirth. The Koran further teaches that God creates from nothing (*ex nihilo*). "All that He needs to do, when He wishes a thing, is to say to it 'Be' and it is" (36:82). Al-Kindi taught that God is more than a creator; he is an originator, needing no matter and no time. In maintaining that world and time had a beginning he differed from Aristotle. As for God's addressing something nonexistent, the Moslem philosopher had an explanation: the use of "Be" is allegorical. This device he developed in another connection. When his puzzled pupil Ahmad raised a question about the meaning of "The stars and the trees offer worship" (sur. 55:6), al-Kindi explained that "offer worship" simply meant that all animate and inanimate objects follow throughout their lives and being divine laws. He thereby suggested a new way of interpreting scriptural material the allegorical way. This was pursued by later thinkers and reformers up to the present day. In their struggle for the Moslem mind, al-Kindi's successors made full use of the powerful weapons that could be forged from interpreting troublesome koranic passages.

This pioneer Arab philosopher was a generalist. He developed no system of his own. He conceived his mission to be transmitting and expounding on the legacy of the ancient Greeks. His contribution was the preservation and presentation of their philosophy. He provided Greek philosophy with a home in Arab culture, blazed the trail for harmony between it and theology, and facilitated the possibility of further accord.

But al-Kindi was more than a philosopher. He was encyclopedic in his knowledge and prodigious in his authorship in many fields. At the 1962 millenary anniversary held in his honor in Baghdad, a researcher presented a list of three hundred sixty-one titles ascribed to him. Of these, twenty-seven were philosophic, twenty-two psychological, twenty-two medical, and the rest mathematical, musical, astronomical, geographical, political, and physical. An Italian scholar of the sixteenth century, Geronimo Cardono, listed al-Kindi among the twelve great minds in history. His book on optics (*al-Manazir*) reintroduced this science into Europe and benefited among others Roger Bacon. Al-Kindi's work on music was one of the earliest extant. Five of his astrological treatises were translated early into Latin and made him known in Europe primarily as an astrologer. Four of his scientific studies, headed by *Fi al-'Aql* (*De intellectu*), were translated by Gerard of Cremona. Ironically, more of al-Kindi's works survived in Latin than in Arabic.

II

THE philosophic venture initiated by the Arab al-Kindi was pursued by al-Farabi, a Turk, and was brought to a grand finale by ibn-Sina, a

Persian. All three wrote their works in Arabic. Sandwiched between al-Kindi and al-Farabi was al-Razi (d. 925), whose extremist views on religion rendered him ineffectual. Al-Razi considered all prophets, from Jesus to Muhammad, impostors and all theologies unworthy of consideration. Unlike al-Kindi he, following Aristotle, considered matter eternal, which was a heresy in Islam. But al-Farabi (d. 950) never incurred the ulama's anathema. His writings were politically rather than religiously oriented and earned him the enviable title of "the second teacher," coming after the great Stagirite. As a philosopher al-Farabi is best known for two books: *Risalah fi Ara' Ahl al-Madinah al-Fadilah* ("an epistle on the opinions of the superior city's people"), modeled after Plato's *Republic*; and *al-Siyasah al-Madaniyah* ("the political regime"), inspired by Aristotle's *Politics*. His model city is conceived as a hierarchical organism comparable to the human body. The ruler, corresponding to the heart, is served by officials who are themselves served by others lower in the hierarchy. The ruler is perfect intellectually and morally. The aim of the organism is solely the welfare of all its members. Moslems came to identify this ideal state with Islam.

Al-Farabi made a major contribution in another field which interested Arab philosophers — music. In fact he is generally acknowledged as the leading musical theorist the Arabs produced. His writings were studied by ibn-Sina and other writers on this subject.

In ibn-Sina (980–1037) Arab philosophy reached its climactic point, as did Arab medicine. The prince of physicians was also the prince of philosophers. His interest in philosophy he owed to his predecessor al-Farabi, whom he in due course overshadowed. After mastering in his teens all available knowledge of the Koran, linguistics, mathematics, and natural sciences, the self-assured scholar tackled Aristotle's *Metaphysics* and for once was baffled. The fortieth reading was no easier than the first, and he gave up in despair. But one day at the urgent entreaties of a bookdealer he reluctantly bought a book by al-Farabi on the subject. That signified the beginning of a new direction in his intellectual career. Thereafter his lifework was divided between philosophy and medicine, with political duties intruding also. In a dozen Samanid and Buwayhid courts the philosopher-physician visited, he often acted as counselor if not vizir, but his performance in politics was as disappointing as his intellectual performance was gratifying.

Ibn-Sina studied the Aristotelian, Platonic, Neoplatonic, and Stoic systems of the West as well as the religious beliefs and systems proposed by wise men of the East. He followed none consistently but endeavored to integrate elements from all into a system of his own. The one he finally structured was the first of its kind in Islam, a comprehensive one involving God, man, and the universe as they operate independently and interrelatedly.

God, according to the Sinaic system, exists. His existence is identical with his being. He is the only necessary being, unique and transcendent. His attributes of power and knowledge are identical with his essence as an unchanging being. He causes but is not caused, changes but is not changed. Clearly this God is not the Aristotelian God, who neither created the world nor is concerned with it. He is the Semitic deity reformulated in philosophic terms. He differs from the Islamic God in the rational interpretation of his attributes and in his creativity. Creation was not *ex nihilo*. Matter was eternal (*qadim*) and the process was limited in neither time nor place. It was rather one of emanation as a consequence of his will and being. Active intelligence was the first to emanate, followed by the soul and the body. This Creator does not keep direct contact with the created.

Other than God all beings are possible, as opposed to necessary. As such they require, as a prerequisite for existence, a being which can only be obtained through God. The following is the logic he employed, which was in time passed through Maimonides (ibn-Maymun) and Thomas Aquinas to the Jewish and Christian scholastic philosophies:

> Every series arranged in the order of causes and effects — whether finite or infinite — if it includes only what is caused, clearly needs an external cause linked to it at one end of the series. It is equally clear that if the series does not include anything uncaused, this is the end of the series, its limit. Every series therefore ends at the Being, who is necessary by Himself.[1]

[1] *Al-Isharat w-al-Tanbihat*, ed. Sulayman Dunya (Cairo, 1958), parts 3–4, p. 455. Cf. Philip K. Hitti, *Makers of Arab History* (New York and London, 1968), p. 211.

This Sinaic argument, that all possible beings require for their existence a necessary Being existing by himself, is still used as a proof of the existence of God.

Man, ibn-Sina taught, is made up of two substances: soul and body. Soul is a substance in itself. Its substantiality relates to its immortality and entails the continuous existence of the individual mind. Bodily resurrection, with its delights, taught in unmistakable words in the Koran, cannot be rationally explained and is therefore categorically denied. Pertinent passages should therefore be allegorically interpreted; they are meant to accommodate the masses.

Prophethood, a more fundamental institution in Islam than in Christianity, was accepted in name but redefined and modified in function. The prophet is not one endowed and ordained by God to act as his spokesman, but a man with human — not superhuman — qualities produced by society to lead in the solution of its problems. In a society there are a variety of members with differing intellectual and moral capabilities. The leader-prophet has the advantage of a superior intuition, to appreciate the needs and problems of the community; a vivid imagination, to project satisfying solutions; and persuasive powers, to present his message in a convincing way. His message has political and social aspects. He may establish contact with the "active intelligence," a transcendental intelligence — whether potential, actual, or acquired — distinct from the human intellect and corresponding to the Christian Holy Ghost or the Judeo-Muslim Gabriel. But prophetic knowledge remains internal. Aware of the attractiveness of sensuous pleasures to the ordinary man, the prophet addresses him in allegorical and symbolic language. This the ordinary man takes in its literal sense — but not the intellectual man. By way of implementing his mission this leader-prophet prescribes prayers, fasting, and pilgrimage at stated times.

Ibn-Sina's justification of his addiction to wine is revealing. "By religious law wine is illegal for the fool; by intellectual law it is legal for the intelligent." In his youthful days, according to his own story, he began to use wine to keep awake during his long nights of study.

Free will was another vexatious philosophic-religious problem tackled by this philosopher. The dilemma it posed had provided exercise for many thinkers before ibn-Sina, and it still does. If human beings are controlled by divinely imposed necessity, they are not responsible for wrongdoing and should not be punished for it by a just God. If they are not controlled, God's sovereignty is compromised. In Islam the controversy is complicated by the clearly expressed koranic doctrine of predestination. This doctrine has a double aspect: God's universal, eternal decree (*qada'*), and the application of the decree in time and place and to a particular individual (*qadar*). This makes God the direct cause of whatever happens to man. The Koran is explicit on this point and its commentators are wholeheartedly committed to it.

As one committed to logical reasoning ibn-Sina had no choice. He had to concede human freedom of will to justify man's responsibility entailing reward or punishment, in accordance with the law of cause and effect. Again he incurred the theologian's ban. His denial of predestination was as abhorrent as his denial of bodily resurrection and his acceptance of the world's eternity. Hard as he tried, this Moslem philosopher could not be true to Islam and to philosophy. His allegiance had to lie either with Mecca and Medina or with Athens and Alexandria. The interpretation he gave may have satisfied him, but not his adversaries. Like al-Kindi before him and ibn-Rushd after him, ibn-Sina was simply declared an atheist (*kafir*). At the instigation of theologians an 'Abbasid caliph (al-Mustanjid, d. 1170) ordered his books burned. It was ibn-Sina's philosophy rather than his science that condemned him in the eyes of his coreligionists.

The magisterial work of ibn-Sina in philosophy was strangely titled *al-Shifa'* ("healing"), its abridgment *al-Najah* ("deliverance"). In size and significance of the role it played, *al-Shifa'* is comparable to *al-Qanun*. Recently published in six volumes (Cairo, 1952–65), it is perhaps the largest work on philosophy by any one man. It begins with logic and includes physics and metaphysics, geology and meteorology, botany and zoology, mathematics and music, and psychology. Astrology is rejected. Logic, originally a Greek science, was received with marked enthusiasm by Moslems and abundantly used in their sectarian disputes. Ibn-Sina did not limit his study of logic to Aristotle's *Organon*. He wrote *Mantiq al-Mashriqiyin* ("the logic of Orientals"), perhaps intended to form part of his *al-Hikmah al-Mashriqiyah* ("Oriental wisdom").

In another major philosophic work, *al-Isharat w-al-Tanbihat* ("directions and notices"), the author devoted three chapters to Sufism, in addition to his thirty-two other works on the subject. Though generally sympathetic, his treatment was objective. Asceticism to him was not enough: he believed one should seek illumination as the final act of knowledge. Illumination is available through the angels acting as a liaison between the celestial and the terrestrial spheres. The doctrine of illumination was an amalgam of Near Eastern (particularly Persian) and Greek (particularly Neoplatonic) elements. It relates to that of gnosis, which has been treated in the chapter on Sufism. Ibn-Sina can therefore be said to have opened the way for a new brand of Sufi philosophy, the illuminative one (*hikmat al-ishraq*), inaugurated by his follower al-Suhrawardi (d. 1191).

The influence of ibn-Sina's original thinking was manifest not only in the works of his followers but in those of his detractors. Traces of Sinaic thinking are discernible in the writings of his liberal coreligionists down to the present day. The learned Syrian Christian ibn-al-'Ibri (d. 1286) rendered parts of *al-Shifa'* into Syriac and followed Sinaic views on the soul. *Al-Najah* was translated by ibn-Sina himself into his native tongue and was responsible for introducing philosophy with its Arabic vocabulary into Persian. In the 1950s three millenary (according to the lunar calendar) celebrations were held in ibn-Sina's honor by Persians, Turks, and Arabs. The Turks claimed him because of his father's birthplace Balkh, where Turkish and Persian were spoken. The Teheran and Baghdad celebrations were distinguished by including participants from four continents. A feature of the Teheran celebration was unveiling ibn-Sina's statue at Hamadhan, where he once lived and where a new tomb for him was built. Among other publications prompted by these occasions was a bibliography of his works including two hundred seventy-six titles of which two hundred have survived. This makes ibn-Sina a competitor of al-Kindi's for being the most prolific Arabic author.

The philosophical works of ibn-Sina were rendered into Latin, where he became known as Avicenna (the name probably came into

129

Latin from Hebrew, where the Arabic *b* is pronounced like *v*). His *al-Shifa'* was wrongly translated in certain editions as *Sufficientia.* The reception his writings received is indicative of the favorable intellectual climate of the time. Their relevance did not escape religious thinkers. Here was a philosopher who dealt with the same general problem of adjusting Greek concepts to monotheistic belief, a problem which, with its paradoxes, had for the first time been intensively agitating scholastic minds. His approach and method could serve as a model and his solutions might suggest other possible ones, despite the fact that such doctrines as the Trinity and Christ's resurrection and transubstantiation presented problems unique to Christianity.

A German Dominican, Albertus Magnus (Albert the Great, d. 1280), was one of the early scholastics to interest himself in Arab philosophic works as he attempted to integrate Aristotelianism with Christian theology. Albertus studied at Cologne and taught there and at Paris. He included among his students an Italian, Thomas Aquinas (d. 1274), destined to outstrip his teacher. In his writings, particularly *Summa Theologiae,* Thomas Aquinas systematized Catholic theology and left a philosophic system that became known as Thomism. His extensive use of Avicenna is attested to by the hundreds of references he made to him. Though often he quotes to criticize, traces of Sinaic influence are clear not only in the proof of God's existence he presents but in various other doctrines. Through this "prince of the scholastics," as Thomas Aquinas was called, Arab philosophy established a foothold in Western culture. On the whole Avicenna looked tolerable to the Europeans: he believed in one God and in creation, prophecy, and immortality. Dante was so considerate as to assign him to limbo, the abode of souls which missed the Christian revelation.

On the Continent, Cologne and Paris became centers of Arab studies; in the British Isles, Oxford. The celebrated philosopher and man of science Roger Bacon (d. 1294) studied at both Paris and Oxford and served in Oxford as a Franciscan monk. He evidently knew Hebrew as well as Arabic and was one of the best informed medievalists on ibn-Sina. He ranked him greatest after Aristotle. Another British scholar, Duns Scotus (d. 1308), studied and lectured at Oxford and in Paris and came under Arab influence, as is reflected in his many writings.

The question has often been raised, How creative was the thinking of ibn-Sina and his coreligionist colleagues? Some have claimed that Arab philosophy was a series of footnotes to Plato and Aristotle. But creativity based on nothing takes place only in theology. The creative process presupposes the existence of old elements which when combined in new ways or with new elements yield a new and useful product. In this case Arab creativity consisted in combining old philosophic and theologic ideas to produce original and useful ones. True, certain ideas did not achieve popular acceptance, but their effect on the liberal heritage of man is unmistakable. Ibn-Sina isolated and defined the problems in the conflict between philosophy and theology and he offered original solutions, leaving it to others to improve on them if possible.

With ibn-Sina the process of translation and origination initiated two centuries earlier under al-Ma'mun came to an abrupt end. Intellectual activity thereafter was channeled into theological matters. Al-Ghazzali's critique of philosophers may have contributed to this result but the determining factors were more political and socioeconomic. Happily, however, as the sun of philosophy waned in the East it waxed in the West, reaching its meridian in ibn-Rushd, an Arab follower of ibn-Sina and native of Spain.

III

EARLY Spanish Islam looked back to the motherland for spiritual as well as intellectual guidance and inspiration. There were various channels of communication. The holy pilgrimage provided a natural means. Young seekers after learning took advantage of the opportunity to join circles of shaykhs in the mosques of Mecca and Medina and at times in Baghdad and Damascus. Student migration was another means. Graduates of schools in Cordova, Seville, Toledo, and other cities sought to do their graduate work in the colleges of Hijaz, Iraq, and Syria with the same eagerness that characterizes present-day Near Eastern students seeking their education in Western European and

American universities. Professors migrated too, but in the reverse direction. Some were invited to universities in Spain, others were attracted there. In the golden age of the Umayyad caliphate at Cordova (929–1027) the movement acquired the proportions of a modern-day "brain drain." The importation of books was another channel through which learning flowed westward. Books formed more than a small part of the east-to-west caravan freight.

Philosophy predictably was not an early import into Spanish Islam. Theology and science were not contaminated by ibn-Sina's brand of philosophy for a couple of centuries.

The first Moslem philosopher to surface on Spanish soil was a Cordovan, ibn-Masarrah, who died in 931, a half-century after al-Kindi. Ibn-Masarrah advocated a system fathered by the Sicilian-Greek philosopher Empedocles but was better known as an esoteric mystic. He introduced and propagated the concepts of illuminative philosophy. The philosophy he founded realized its most distinguished exponent in ibn-'Arabi of Seville (d. 1240), the greatest speculative genius of Sufism. Ibn-'Arabi combined Sufism and pantheism in a central theme he designated (as noted earlier) "the unity of existence" (*wahdat al-wujud*). All things, he taught, preexist as ideas in the knowledge of God, from which they emanate and to which they return. The famous Jewish philosopher of Malaga ben-Gabirol (Avicebron, d. ca. 1058) shared with ibn-Masarrah the salient features of pseudo-Empedoclean philosophy and, more importantly, became the first Jewish teacher of Neoplatonism in the West. A millennium earlier another Jew, Philo of Alexandria, had Orientalized Neoplatonism, preparatory to its Christianization and Islamization, and now in the form of Greco-Arab philosophy, Neoplatonism was reintroduced into Europe.

Of special interest is another philosopher, ibn-Tufayl (d. 1185), whose connection with ibn-Sina was literary and with ibn-Rushd, personal. Like his distinguished predecessor ibn-Sina and his successor ibn-Rushd, ibn-Tufayl was a physician, philosopher, and courtier. He practiced medicine at Granada and politics at the Muwahhid court in Morocco (Marrakush). The literary legacy he left bears the same title as ibn-Sina's mystic allegory *Hayy ibn-Yaqzan* ("the living, son of the vigilant"), but the contents are entirely his own creation.

The story's hero, Hayy, is born spontaneously on a barren islet in the middle of the Indian Ocean. He is brought up by a deer. In due course the lone figure differentiates himself from his fellow quadrupeds and realizes his superiority. The death of the deer suggests to him the difference between body and what makes body alive. Finally he comes to the realization that in man there is a soul, incorruptible and immortal, and above man a god, all-wise and all-knowing. Moral: even if deprived of the benefit of parents and teachers, one can through reason and common sense arrive at knowledge of the ultimate truth — in this case orthodox Islam.

The originality and charm of the story gave it wide appeal in Europe and Asia. Published (1671) in Arabic and in Latin by Edward Pocock, the first professor of Arabic at Oxford University, the story became a best seller. The author's first name, abu-Bakr, was corrupted into Abubacer, by which the Latins came to know him. In 1672 a Dutch translation appeared and two years later an English one by a Quaker. Quakers found in it support for their belief in the "inner light." In 1708 there was another English translation (by S. Ockley) and in 1761 a German rendition was made. Interest in the book did not cease. A Russian translation appeared in 1920 and a Spanish one in 1934. The story inspired other works. Hayy was obviously a forerunner of Defoe's Robinson Crusoe and Rousseau's Emile.

Ibn-Tufayl spent the last days of his life as court physician and counselor to the second Muwahhid sultan, abu-Ya'qub Yusuf, at Morocco. This dynasty, like its Murabit predecessor, was of Berber origin and a successor to the Umayyad caliphate of Cordova. Abu-Ya'qub dabbled in philosophy. He emulated Harun and al-Ma'mun in patronizing the learned, and he dreamed of making Morocco the Baghdad of Western Islam. Before his death in 1185 ibn-Tufayl introduced and recommended to his patron a young scholarly friend, ibn-Rushd.

IV

ABU-AL-WALID MUHAMMAD IBN-RUSHD was born (1126) in Cordova into a family of jurisconsults. Both his father and his grandfather had held the office of chief judge in the capital city at a time when it was the leading intellectual center in Spain and a leading one in Europe. Abu-al-Walid attended its mosque-based university and specialized in law and medicine, the only two sciences considered to require high intellectual ability. With medicine went philosophy, both listed in the curriculum under one title, *hikmah*.

After practicing his double profession in his birthplace, the young physician-jurist moved to Morocco, where he was favored with the patronage of abu-Ya'qub Yusuf. The sultan commissioned the scholar to prepare a simplified and meaningful text on philosophy. The commission carried with it an honorarium, a robe of honor, and an appointment as chief justice, first in Seville and then in Cordova. In 1182 the enlightened ruler invited his protégé to occupy the same position held by ibn-Tufayl, a position he continued to hold under abu-Ya'qub's son al-Mansur.

The cordial relationship between the new patron and his protégé was interrupted in 1194 when the king sent the sixty-eight-year-old scholar into exile and ordered the burning of his books. The reason for the unexplained action is not difficult to unearth. Theologians exerted pressure to have the philosopher considered a traitor to his religion and consequently to his society. Ibn-Rushd's attempt to keep one foot in Islam while reaching with the other into the realm of philosophy was no more successful than ibn-Sina's or al-Kindi's. Two years later, however, the expatriate was reinstated in royal favor, but it was too late. Humiliated and heartbroken over the destruction of his books, the aged philosopher died on December 10, 1198. His remains were later removed to Cordova.

What writings of ibn-Rushd were lost to the world by the royal fire is unascertainable. Fortunately, however, his scientific works were spared and, with his philosophic works that survived, constitute a rich legacy. Of his medical books the most valuable is *al-Kulliyat fi al-Tibb* ("generalities in medicine," wrongly translated into Latin as *Colliget*, a corrupted form of the Arabic). The *Kulliyat* is an encyclopedic composition covering anatomy, physiology, materia medica, disease, hygiene, and therapeutics. Good as it was, it had no chance of survival in competition with ibn-Sina's *Canon*. Among its original contributions was a recognition of the possibility of immunity in such diseases as smallpox and the realization that the function of the retina is to transmit images to the brain.

Ibn-Rushd the philosopher was more influential than ibn-Rushd the physician. His contribution in the former role was the simplification of philosophy with which his first patron had entrusted him. It involved rendering complicated thoughts of alien people, worked out over a thousand years earlier in a foreign language, intelligible and relevant to his Arab Moslem contemporaries. Ibn-Rushd knew no Greek. He first studied carefully and critically Arabic translations of Aristotle's works and their relation to commentaries on them by Greek or Arab authors. Then he proceeded with his presentation, which took the form of a commentary. The commentary was directed at three levels — beginning, intermediate, advanced — and took three corresponding forms. For beginners the commentary (entitled *talkhis*, "epitome"), was a quasi-original composition, summarizing, paraphrasing, explaining, and rearranging the original material and even mixing it with data from other sources. For advanced study the commentary (*tafsir, sharh*, "the real one") was longer and different in form from talkhis. Here the original was quoted and was kept apart from the explanation, which was usually longer than that in talkhis and followed the original more closely. One paragraph after another was so treated in order. The model was obviously supplied by the usual koranic exegesis. The commentator considered it his duty to purge Aristotle of accretions, disentangle Aristotelianism from Neoplatonism, and fill lacunae. The intermediate commentary (*jawami', summa*, "compendium") naturally fell between the other two. It used direct quotations sparingly, amplifying and clarifying when necessary.

Of the thirty-eight commentaries ibn-Rushd wrote, thirty-six survived in Hebrew, thirty-four in Latin, and only twenty-eight in Arabic. Jews had no Hebrew translation of Aristotle, so they depended on Arabic translations and Arabic commentaries. Within fifty years after his death, Averroes, to use his Latin name (as it came from the Hebrew), became known as "the great commentator," and Averroism, his brand of philosophy, achieved currency.

Ibn-Rushd was indeed more than a commentator. To the problem of harmony between religion and philosophy he dedicated a book titled *Fasl al-Maqal* ("the decisive treatise"). For God's existence he offered the proof of causality as it relates to what is possible or contingent and what is necessary. The theory of emanation he rejected. Matter in the Rushdite view is eternal. The creative process is one of self-renewal operating in perpetuity. In this he anticipated the modern theory of evolution. As a devotee of rational reasoning and demonstrative truth, ibn-Rushd could not accept the theological doctrine of predestination or of corporeal resurrection. God's knowledge differs from man's. It causes but is not caused. God's knowledge of details is no more than a governor's direct knowledge of the detailed execution of an administrative act.

The soul, in the Rushdite view, is immortal, and the delights of Paradise are not sensuous. Plato's ideal state is accepted with reservations. It comes about through a prophet-legislator. Its citizenry comprises three classes: the upper, the ruling class, follows demonstrative truth; the lowest, the commonalty, is persuaded by rhetoric and allegory as used by preachers; in between lies the middle group, responsive to the dialectic arguments of theologians. Thus is truth structured on three levels. The necessity for maintaining a double-standard truth was felt by other teachers and exists in embryonic form in Christ's teaching (Matt. 13:10–1).

The Latinization of Arab philosophy that began with al-Kindi and continued with ibn-Sina reached its high point with ibn-Rushd. His thought worked its way into the fabric of Jewish and Christian medieval philosophy. The Hebrew translations of his commentaries, started in Naples in 1232, and the Latin ones, initiated by Michel Scot in 1220 under the auspices of Frederick II of Sicily, were repeatedly revised and kept in vogue. In the 1470s more than fifty editions appeared in Venice. Thomas Aquinas made extensive use of Averroes' writings, often noting his disapproval of them. Averroism established itself in due course in the curricula of major European universities. Its popularity aroused clerics' ire as Rushdism had aroused the ulamas'. In 1210 the Paris council banned its study. In 1231 a papal injunction did likewise. But banned or not the Averroist rational strain found its way into the universal stream of liberalism.

With ibn-Rushd the line of Arab philosophers in the West came to an end. The Cordovan philosopher left no followers. The movement inaugurated over three and a half centuries earlier in distant Baghdad breathed its last on Andalusian soil.

V

IT IS often remarked disparagingly that the Arabs were transmitters. From the standpoint of the history of thought transmission is not necessarily less important than origination. For instance, if the Decalogue, the Sermon on the Mount, or the first surah of the Koran had not been transmitted, what use would they have been? Their effectiveness would have been limited in time and place. But the Arabs were much more than transmitters; they were interpreters and preservers. In addition to the role they played in the recovery of the Greek intellectual tradition and its absorption into the Latin West, they made, as indicated above, original contributions in the marginal zone where philosophy and religion meet, contributions that transcended Islam to involve its two sister religions.

LITERATURE

◆◆◆ THE word "literature" may be used in a broad, or etymological, sense to include any writing that has come to us from the past. Especially in the case of remote or little-known civilizations, a clay tablet, a parchment, or a stone bearing a marriage contract, a business transaction, or a medical prescription can be considered literature. In a more limited meaning, literature comprises writings that convey the highest thoughts or deepest emotions of a people expressed in poetry or elegant prose. Literary compositions are then only those which in form or content have aesthetic value. The Arabic word for "literature," *adab*, can also be used in this dual sense. In this study, however, literature is used only in the latter sense.

Arabic literature, like the civilization to which it is a monument, is not the product of one people, but the product at different times of various peoples — Moslems and non-Moslems, whites and nonwhites — spread from Spain through North Africa to eastern Asia. It is inter-religious and interracial. It is one of the richest legacies of its kind, which left a marked influence on Persian, Turkish, Urdu, and other literatures. It has also left its mark on European literatures. It is called "Arabic" simply because Arabic was the medium through which it was expressed.

I

THIS literature sprang into being about A.D. 500 with an outpouring of poetry from North Arabia, particularly Najd. It is not surprising that poetry rather than prose was the form it took in view of the fact that man feels before he reasons; poetry therefore precedes prose. The surprise is that the poetry was mature and polished in form and content. The theme was already conventionalized and the technique traditionalized, suggesting a long period of development in the art of imaginative expression. Not only was Arabic poetry the earliest form of literary expression, it was also the most highly prized and most enduring form.

The form that typifies this pre-Islamic production was *qasidah*, an ode consisting of couplets following a specific meter. The couplets vary in number from fifteen to a hundred and twenty and end in the same rhyme. The meter in Arabic is measured not by stress but by the number and length of syllables. From this ancient age, called "the heroic age," over a hundred qasidahs have survived. They mirror as nothing else does the Bedouin life of pre-Islam (*jahiliyah*) with its razzias and vendettas and its tribal feuds and wars. The poet was the chronicler, journalist, and public-relations man of his tribe. He was also its oracle and champion. He kept the genealogies of his people, extolled their virtues, and recited their military exploits, in which he often took part. To the extent the poet aggrandized his tribesmen, he belittled and satirized their rivals. His emergence in a community was one of the three most joyous occasions, the other two being the birth of a boy and the foaling of a purebred mare.

The poet's unwritten compositions were memorized and it was said they "flew across the desert faster than arrows"; they were also passed on from one generation to another. The flight could not have been very fast, however, since the most popular poems were not recorded until the second and third centuries after Islam.

The ode is in fact a monodrama. The actor is the poet and he is, of course, always the hero. The prelude is usually short and amatory, stating the name of a beloved — mostly fictitious — and a description of her beauty. It is followed by an account of a visit to the maiden's camping ground, which is found vacant. The poem next shows the hero en route presumably in search for the maiden but really in quest of a patron. In this section the poet describes his horse and his hunting forays, and perhaps he ends the poem with a tale of his victorious encounter with a foe.

Of the pre-Islamic odes that have survived, seven hold a unique place of honor. Legend asserts that each in its turn won the annual prize at the fair of 'Ukaz near Taif. The fair provided the tribesmen of the area with the opportunity of exhibiting their agricultural and industrial products as well as their poetical compositions. The winning ode was supposedly inscribed in golden letters and suspended on the Kaabah wall; hence the name of the book of surviving odes — *Seven Mu'allaqat* ("suspended").

An especially interesting mu'allaqah was one by 'Antar ('Antarah) ibn-Shaddad (ca. 525–615), a poet, knight, warrior, and lover. 'Antar was denied citizenship by the sons of the desert — whose pride in ancestry made them trace theirs uninterruptedly to Adam — because 'Antar's mother was a black slave, possibly an Ethiopian Christian. He was one of the many famous "ravens [*aghribah*] of the Arabs." What made the rejection more painful was his unrewarded love for his beautiful cousin 'Ablah. As a cousin he had first claim to her, but a free woman could not marry a slave. This further rejection spurred him to achieve a reputation for valor, but it availed him nothing. Dispirited, he sulked. At the next encounter with an enemy tribe he refused to take part.

"Charge!" ordered his father.

"The slave is not for fighting," 'Antar replied. "He is for milking camels."

"Charge!" repeated his father. "You are free."

Happily he was then able to marry his sweetheart, and he rose to the headship of the tribe.

'Antar's death was worthy of his legendary life. Fatally wounded in battle by a poisoned shaft, he nevertheless remounted his horse, and by propping himself up on his lance he kept the enemy from knowing the true state of his condition and thus ensured the safe retreat of his tribesmen. None dared approach him until by a cunning device the horse was startled and the corpse fell. In two couplets of his mu-'allaqah he addresses his beloved 'Ablah:

> Of thee I thought midst thirsty spears,
>> Midst swordblades dripping with my blood.
> I fain would kiss those shining sword tips,
>> For they recalled thy smiling lips.[1]

Other verses 'Antar sang in praise of his military prowess established a pattern of self-glorification bearing his name — 'Antariyat — that was followed by later poets:

> I have resolution firmer than rock,
>> stronger than mountains unmovable.
> I have a sword with which if I strike time,
>> it separates it entirely from its past.
> I have a shining lance that on a dark night
>> could guide me and prevent me from going astray.
> I have a fast steed whenever he speeds,
>> his striking hooves let fly lightning sparks.
> Dark of color, he splits the starless night
>> but for a white crescent-like spot between his eyes.
> He ransoms me with his life on the battlefield
>> and I ransom him with mine and whatever I possess.[2]

Around the name of 'Antar, the paragon of Arab chivalry, a whole cycle of heroic deeds has been woven by storytellers from the ninth century through the reign of Mamluks during the Crusades. As the original legend passed into neighboring lands, including Persia and India, it gained fresh and strange material. The black knight of the desert and heathen Arabia became the knight of Islam. His romance (qissah, sirah) still fascinates listeners in the cafés of Baghdad, Cairo, and Beirut. In Arabic it served as a model for other romances. At the turn of the nineteenth century 'Antar was introduced into France and

---

[1] Abd-al-Mun'im 'A. Shalabi, Sharh Diwan 'Antarah ibn-Shaddad (Cairo, 1960), p. 150. Cf. Anne and Wilfrid S. Blunt, The Seven Golden Odes of Pagan Arabia (London, 1903), pp. 33 et seq., although these particular verses are not found there.

[2] Cf. Arthur J. Arberry, Arabic Poetry: A Primer for Students (Cambridge, Eng., 1965), pp. 36–7, where another translation and the Arabic version are given.

achieved a vogue in Western Europe. In 1910 his story was adapted for the stage by Shukri Ghanim, a Lebanese living in Paris.

As 'Antar personified the early Arab ideals of valor and love, Hatim al-Ta'i (d. ca. 605) personified the ideals of generosity and hospitality, and like 'Antar he became a partly historical, partly legendary figure. Hatim was born to his mother's order: while pregnant she was given the choice in a dream between having a son endowed with courage and one endowed with liberality, and she had no difficulty making up her mind. She chose the latter. As a boy Hatim would not eat his food unless he shared it with other boys. As a lad in charge of the family's herd, he considered it his duty to slaughter three camels to feed passing strangers. For that he was expelled from the tribe. He visited Hirah and other places, singing the praises of liberality and unselfishness. Even after his death Hatim was not to disappoint a supplicant. When his daughter was led as a captive before the Prophet she recited anecdotes about her father, and the Prophet reportedly remarked, "Let her go. Her father loved noble manners, and so does God." No more flattering epithet could today be bestowed upon a man than to call him a "Hatim."

Arabic literature is replete with tales about Hatim's proverbial generosity, but nowhere is he made the hero of a romance. This was left to Persian literature, from which it was passed on to Urdu, Tatar, and Turkish. The printed collection of his poems (*Diwan*) comprises several compositions written by him.

II

ENTER Islam, exit jahiliyah poetry. Its general association with heathenism was enough to condemn it. In his zeal to wean his people from their paganism, Muhammad frowned on many practices of its followers. Besides, since poets were generally believed to be quasi-prophets, possessed of some superhuman power, Muhammad must have felt they were in competition with him. His denunciatory contrast of the two categories suggests this:

> Shall I tell you upon whom Satans descend?
> They descend upon every guilty liar.
> They listen, but most of them falsely speak.

As for the poets, the beguiled follow them.
Seest thou not that in whatever they treat
    they go astray,
And that they say what they do not do?
(26:221–6)

With Islam the Muse turned her back on the desert and sought urban centers for her habitat — Medina, Damascus, Baghdad, and Cairo. In her new abode the goddess changed her garb and assumed new attributes in response to changed religious, political, and socio-economic conditions. The migration did not end until al-Andalus was reached. The tribe or shaykh as patron was replaced by the caliph, sultan, or amir.

The first believing poet was a Medinese-born convert, Hassan ibn-Thabit. Hassan was seven years Muhammad's senior and did not embrace the new faith until late in his life. He had participated in the 'Ukaz poetical tournament and lost the prize to a Bedouin rival. The Prophet assigned him the double duty of responding to the bards who served as spokesmen for the tribal deputations rushing to offer submission to the Prophet after his victory at al-Hudaybiyah, and of responding to the lampoons of unbelieving poets. As a token of appreciation, Muhammad presented his poet laureate with a slave girl, a sister of Mariyah, his Coptic concubine. Though a second-rate poet with no distinction in imaginativeness or style, Hassan won undying honor for singing the glories of the master and of Islam. His verse is studded with koranic phraseology, and his name stands for the father of religious poetry.

The trio who dominated poetry in the Umayyad period of Damascus had mercenary rather than religious motivation. The first to emerge was al-Akhtal (Ghiyath ibn-al-Salt, ca. 640–710) of the Christian tribe of Taghlib in the neighborhood of Hirah. Al-Akhtal was recommended to the second caliph, Yazid, as the one to boost the new Umayyad regime (late converts to Islam) at the expense of the Ansar (early converts). So effective were his poems that they aroused a storm in Medina. The caliph shared with the poet his royal food and wine; he even took him, a Christian, in his company when he went to Mecca. But it was some time before al-Akhtal was officially appointed court poet. When that time came, however, Caliph 'Abd-al-Malik had his announcer roam the capital's streets with al-Akhtal broadcasting: "This is the poet of the commander of the believers. This is the Arabs' poet." The Arabs' poet persisted in his addiction to wine, turned in prayer to the east (as early Christians did), and kept a golden cross dangling from his neck even in the caliph's presence. When his patron invited him to embrace the state religion he boldly and proudly refused, adding as if in a footnote, "I consent with the proviso that I do not abstain from wine or observe the fast of Ramadan." In fact his Christianity was a matter of formality and external observance. He divorced his wife, married a divorcée, kept company with prostitutes, and drank to saturation, claiming he could not compose poetry otherwise.

Meanwhile the laureate found himself in competition for caliphal favor with a Moslem, Jarir, the champion poet of the tribe domiciled near Kufah. Jarir had his chance to win the caliph's favor when the pious 'Umar II was enthroned. A war of words raged between the two poets. Thus, two stars in the poetical firmament of Damascus turned satirists.

Other types of poetry, mostly amatory, arose at this time in North Arabia. Some of the poets specialized in writing about courtly and Platonic love, a type of poetry that reached its height in Moslem Spain and contributed to the rise of its counterpart in Western poetry. The Meccan poet 'Umar ibn-abi-Rabi'ah (d. ca. 719) sang of the beauty of princesses and of pilgrim damsels to Hijaz. Jamil al-'Udhri (d. 701) addressed to his sweetheart verses rich in pure and innocent love. He wrote about a semimythical contemporary who was so infatuated with Layla that he became crazy (*majnun*). Though she reciprocated his love she was forced by her father to marry another suitor. Only when her name was mentioned would "Majnun Layla" return to his senses. The "Crazy of Layla" became the hero of numberless Arabic, Turkish, and Persian romances extoling the power of undying love.

The first three centuries of the 'Abbasid caliphate (ca. 800–1100) were the golden age not only in science and philosophy but in imaginative literature too. The society was an affluent one, enjoying the blessings and suffering the attendant evils. With luxurious and extravagant living went slaves and concubines, corruption, voluptuousness, and drunkenness. The poetical themes of Damascus and the desert lost their relevance. The time-honored qasidah, index of standard poetry, was laid aside. Reverence to traditional conventions and to old canons of linguistic artistry declined. The classical period of poetry therewith ended and the golden age began.

The poet who personified in his life and verse the spirit of the new age was a Persian-born, Iraqi-educated, Baghdadi resident named abu-Nuwas (Hasan ibn-Hani', ca. 750–814). Abu-Nuwas' father was an Arab, his mother a Persian washerwoman. He enjoyed the protection of the Persian Barmaki viziers at the court of Harun al-Rashid. This gave him entrée into the *Arabian Nights,* where he figures as a jester. He also served al-Amin as a boon companion. Abu-Nuwas was primarily a poet of eroticism and bacchanalia. But the love about which he sang was not Platonic, nor was it usually the love of women. It was the love of boys which he extolled. Hypocrisy was not one of his vices. He boasts in his *Diwan* that not a thing displeasing to God did he fail to commit, unless it was polytheism. For his un-Islamic conduct he was jailed many times, and as many times released — thanks to his poetry.

In his wine songs (*khamriyat*), considered incomparable in Arabic, abu-Nuwas reminds us of 'Umar al-Khayyam:

> Ho! a cup, and fill it up, and tell me it is wine,
> For I will never drink in shade if I can drink
> in shine!
> Curst and poor is every hour that sober I must go,
> But rich am I whene'er well drunk I stagger
> to and fro.
> Speak, for shame, the loved one's name, let vain
> disguise alone:
> No good there is in pleasures o'er which a
> veil is thrown.[3]

Before the end of his life the licentious poet turned ascetic, but the reputation he holds among Arab critics as one of the two greatest Arab poets was certainly not due to the verses composed then.

[3] Reynold A. Nicholson, *A Literary History of the Arabs* (Cambridge, Eng., reprint 1966), p. 295.

The brightest luminary in the entire Arab poetical firmament was presumably abu-al-Tayyib Ahmad al-Mutanabbi, son of a water-carrier of Kufah. A strikingly brilliant student, Ahmad followed his studies in Baghdad and Damascus with a sojourn in the desert, the fount of pure, unadulterated Arabic. He was precocious and he knew it; he not only knew it but exploited it. In his youth he claimed prophecy (which explains his last name, meaning "the would-be prophet"), composed Koran-like surahs, and gained a following as he moved in Syria from one place to another. In Hims he was committed as a heretic to a prison whose doors did not open for him until he recanted.

In 948 al-Mutanabbi gravitated into the Shi'ite court of Sayf-al-Dawlah al-Hamdani, a munificent patron of learning in the way Harun was. The poet himself had Shi'ite leanings of the extremist variety. For nine years al-Mutanabbi served as official poet overshadowing all other poets in the court circle at Aleppo. These were indeed the most fruitful years in his poetical career. He accompanied the ruler on his campaigns against the Byzantines and immortalized them in verse. The patron's munificence was in direct proportion to the poet's encomiums. To the skill of construction and felicity of expression, the master poet added the use of nuggets of wisdom and philosophy that make a number of his verses quotable today as proverbs. The more than forty commentaries on his *Diwan* and other poetical works testify to his enduring popularity.

The following introductory verses of a eulogy addressed to his patron illustrate his style:

> To the resolute, deeds requiring commensurate resolution come;
> > To the noble of character, deeds requiring commensurate nobility come.
> In the eyes of petty actors, petty actions seem magnified;
> > In the eyes of the great, great actions seem minimized.
>
> Sayf-al-Dawlah charges his army with the burden of his ambition,
> > A burden which a multiple army cannot bear.
> Of others he asks no more than he himself feels,
> > A feeling which even lions cannot claim.[4]

[4] For another translation and the original Arabic version see Arberry, *Arabic Poetry*, pp. 84–5.

146

His personality difficulties plagued him again. Estranged from the Hamdanid court he fled with his family to the rival Ikhshidid court of Egypt. The ruler was an especially ugly Negro named Kafur, an ex-slave of the Ikhshidid master whom he had replaced.

The arrogant poet who claimed that the blind could see his literary artistry and the deaf could hear his utterances had nothing in his heart but contempt for the black upstart he eulogized — in expectation of a reward. When that — evidently the governorship of Sidon — was not forthcoming, the panegyrist turned satirist and had to flee to Baghdad. From there he sought a new patron in the Buwayhid sultan of Shiraz. On his way back to Iraq he and his son were murdered by a marauding band of Bedouins.

The last poet of the golden age in the East was Abu-al-'Ala' al-Ma'arri, so named after Ma'arrat al-Nu'man in northern Syria, where he was born in 973 and died in 1058. In his early work he emulated the pattern of al-Mutanabbi's poems but later deviated from it in form and substance. In fact al-Ma'arri was a rare specimen of Moslem poets: he was a pessimistic freethinker. Besides, in his own words, he "never tickled the ears of a potentate with chants or eulogized anyone for mercenary purposes." His pessimism may in part be explained by the total blindness which afflicted him at the age of four after a small-pox attack. He was, however, compensated by his retentive faculty. His frustrating experiences with women, as evidenced by certain verses, must have contributed to making the wine in his blood turn into vinegar. He never married because, as he explained, he did not want to inflict on anyone the wrong his father had inflicted on him.

After a sojourn of a year and a half in Baghdad, where evidently he was inoculated with unorthodox ideas, al-Ma'arri returned home to become what he called "a double prisoner" — a prisoner of blindness and of self-isolation. He practiced asceticism and vegetarianism and limited his activities to teaching, lecturing, and composing. In his *Lu-zumiyat* ("supererogations") the humanist reveals unusual sensitivity to injustice, folly, and vice. He attacks cant and hypocrisy and expresses bold unorthodox religious views:

> Hanifs [Moslems] are stumbling, Christians all astray,
> Jews wildered, Magians far on error's way.

147

We mortals are composed of two great schools —
Enlightened knaves or else religious fools.[5]

The Syrian poet is also known for an ornate prose work, *Risalat al-Ghufran* ("the epistle of forgiveness"). In it he audaciously undertakes a trip to heaven and then hell. In Paradise he interviews poets, many of whom were forgiven unbelievers, freethinkers, and materialists. The Paradise is thus converted into a literary salon in which poets discuss and argue the merits of their compositions. In this work al-Ma-'arri, like his follower ibn-'Arabi (cited in chapter 4), anticipates and affects Dante.

At times the skeptic poet doubted his own doubts, giving his admiring believers a chance to argue that after all he was a believer. In 1944 his thousandth anniversary (lunar years) was celebrated and his tomb was renovated. With al-Ma'arri the golden period of Arab poetry in the East ended, except for a few Sufi compositions, specimens of which have been quoted before. The Sufis developed a new genre of religious poetry — the esoteric. The literary products of their God-intoxicated psalmists come nearest to the Hebrew lyrics.

III

THE Arabs have been called a nation of poets. Wherever they went their poetry was in evidence. To them versification was the hallmark of an educated man. Even today schoolboys try their hands at both verse and prose compositions. In Persia and Spain as well as in Arabia verses in countless numbers poured from high- and low-born to be repeated and admired for their music and exquisite diction if not for their content. The sheer joy in the beauty of words and the euphony of their combinations (referred to above in the chapter on the Koran) maintained its hold on Arabic speakers throughout the ages. No less an intellectual than ibn-Khaldun saw not much in poetry beyond style, meter, and rhyme. One of the glories of 'Ali, an early caliph, was his poetical talent, and the same was true of 'Abd-al-Rahman, the first Moslem ruler of Spain, and of several of his successors.

[5] Nicholson, *Literary History*, p. 318; also cf. Nicholson, *Translations of Eastern Poetry and Prose* (Cambridge, Eng., 1922), p. 110.

Early Western Arab poets, not many of whose productions have been preserved, followed in the footsteps of their Eastern predecessors. But by the early eleventh century new trails in meter and theme had been blazed. Distance from the heartland of Arabism and Islam and contact with an entirely different people and culture in a different physical environment generated an aesthetic climate inhospitable to old ideas and practices solidified in traditional patterns. The poet in the West developed a sensitiveness to the beauty of nature and treated floral, arboreal, and seasonal themes in a manner unknown in the East. He also featured courtly love and tender, romantic sentiment expressed in more refined and polished language. These features were well represented in the works of ibn-Zaydun (abu-al-Walid Ahmad, 1003–71).

Ibn-Zaydun was born in Cordova to a noble family related to the Umayyads. He was a "born poet," having achieved distinction at the age of twenty. Equal distinction came to him as an elegant prose writer. But, as in the case of other poets, he had political ambitions. Unfortunately for him the period was one of the most turbulent in the history of the peninsula with a multiple-contender fight for the heritage of the fallen Umayyad caliphate — involving Arab pretenders fighting among themselves and against Berbers.

Ibn-Zaydun served first as a courtier in Seville but then he moved to Cordova, where he served a jail sentence for political activity. Returning to Seville he assumed a ministry followed by an ambassadorship. Meantime he had fallen desperately in love with Caliph al-Mustakfi's daughter al-Walladah, a poetess in her own right. From prison he addressed to her some of the tenderest poems he ever composed, such as this verse addressed to her at al-Zahra':

> To-day my longing thoughts recall thee here;
> > The landscape glitters, and the sky is clear.
> So feebly breathes the gentle zephyr's gale,
> > In pity of my grief it seems to fail.
> The silvery fountains laugh, as from a girl's
> > Fair throat a broken necklace sheds its pearls.
> Oh, 'tis a day like those of our sweet prime,
> > When, stealing pleasures from indulgent Time,
> We played midst flowers of eye-bewitching hue,
> > That bent their heads beneath the drops of dew.

Alas, they see me now bereaved of sleep;
They share my passion and with me they weep.[6]

But the beautiful and talented princess, the chief attraction in the last days of the Cordovan court, did not reciprocate his love.

Two poetical forms were developed, if not invented, in al-Andalus: *al-muwashshah* and *al-zajal*. Both were lyric, based on a refrain for the chorus, and could be sung to the accompaniment of music. The general theme in both was love.

The muwashshah ("ornamentally girdled") became a highly ornate and stylized form that grew into a veritable literary genre. As an innovation it was the most radical in the history of Arabic poetry. The poem ordinarily comprised ten stanzas, the first having the same rhyme, which is repeated at the end of each succeeding stanza. Though cultivated as a courtly art, the muwashshah allowed for the inclusion of colloquial or even Spanish phrases. The man credited with giving this genre its final form was a blind poet of Tudela, from which came his name al-Tutili (abu-al-'Abbas, d. 1129). The one who did the same for the zajal ("cheer-giving") was a wandering minstrel, ibn-Quzman of Cordova (d. 1160). This bard went from town to town singing the pleasures of love and the praises of the great. It was he who raised the form, till then used only by improvisators and in popular speech, to the dignity of a literary type.

These two typically Andalusian forms, the zajal in particular, aroused the admiration of Spanish Christians and contributed to ethnic assimilation. Their impact is evident on the Castilian popular verse form of *villancico*, extensively used for Christmas songs. From northern Spain the contagion passed into southern France. Provençal poetry appeared full-fledged toward the end of the eleventh century, extoling love, often Platonic, in a wealth of fantastic imagery suggesting Eastern influence. In composition this early poetry followed the meter of ibn-Quzman's poems. In the following centuries those poet-musicians of France and Italy called "troubadours," who are reminiscent of the zajal singers, flourished. Following the Arab precedent the "cult of the dame" arose and spread in Europe.

[6] Nicholson, *Literary History*, p. 425.

Along with lyrical poetry, music passed from Spain into France and Italy. Arab Moslem minstrels, armed with instruments, roamed over the area. Two instruments — the lute and the rebec — contributed immeasurably to the progress of the art of music throughout the Continent. The lute figured prominently as a solo instrument and as part of an orchestral ensemble. An early stringed instrument, the rebec was a progenitor of the viol class. Other instruments whose names betray Arab origin are the guitar, kanoon, and timbal. While minstrels were spreading the art of music, universities in Cordova and other capital cities were teaching musical theories as worked out by al-Kindi, al-Farabi, and ibn-Sina.

IV

LITERARY prose had its start with the Koran. The inimitability associated with the book did not arrest its lasting, incalculable literary influence on subsequent Arabic output. The effect of the King James translation of the Bible on English is slight compared to the effect of the Koran on Arabic. It was the Koran that kept the unity of the language and prevented its fragmentation into dialect.

Secular literary prose entered a new stage with the translation from Pahlawi (Middle Persian) of the Bidpai fables (mentioned in chapter 7) a century and a quarter after the Koran's appearance. Bidpai was a Hindu sage, writing in Sanskrit, who allegedly used his animal tales to instruct his Indian royal patron in practical wisdom and the laws of polity. The Arabic style used by the translator ibn-al-Muqaffa' was simple and lucid and the contents proved charming. The whole was a masterpiece of prose writing. It introduced the short story into Arabic literature and was soon imitated by more than one belletrist. The title Kalilah wa-Dimnah was taken from the names of two jackals who figured in the book, which is still used as a reading text in the schools of the Arab East.

Fiction in the early days of Islam was produced to satisfy human needs by way of instruction or entertainment; in modern times it is written more to describe those needs and to analyze them psychologically. The following is a sample story from the Kalilah:

It is related that a hungry fox came once into a thicket where a drum lay by a tree. As often as the wind moved the branches, they hit the drum and produced a loud noise. Hearing it the fox advanced in its direction, and reaching it he was struck by its huge size. He promised himself a rich repast of meat and fat. After struggling hard he broke the drum apart and discovered that it was hollow, upon which he declared: "The bulkiest and noisiest of things may turn out to be the weakest and most contemptible." [7]

The first European translation of *Kalilah* was into Spanish for King Alfonso the Wise (d. 1284), the patron of Arabic learning. It was followed by Latin translations, which had some vogue in France. Since then, owing to the loss of the Persian translation, the Arabic version has served as the original for translations into more than forty European and Asian languages, including modern Persian. In Arabic the book paved the way for the development of other types of fiction represented by the *maqamah* ("session," "discourse") and *Alf Laylah wa-Laylah* ("a thousand and one nights").

In the maqamah Arab proclivity for ornate composition reached its highest expression. The maqamah is a highly elaborate and affected form describing a dramatized anecdote in rhymed and rhythmic prose interspersed with poetry. The theme is the adventure of a vagabond hero, learned and witty. The author leaves the impression that his main concern is a display of his linguistic dexterity in juggling words and playing on metaphors. The performance seems like one of verbal legerdemain, but below the thick verbiage one might detect a lurking social, economic, or cultural issue.

The inventor of the genre was a Persian born in 968 at Hamadhan. A poet and elegant writer, Ahmad al-Hamadhani went from court to court — Buwayhid, Samanid, Ghaznawid — seeking patronage. He died age forty at Harat (Hirat), where he was eulogizing the great sultan Mahmud of Ghaznah. Fifty-two of his maqamahs survived. So impressed were Arabs by his composition that they bestowed on him the honorific title *Badi' al-Zaman* ("the wonder of the age"), by which he is still known.

---

[7] *Kalilah wa-Dimnah*, ed. L. Cheikho, 2nd ed. (Beirut, 1923), p. 55. Cf. Philip K. Hitti, *Islam and the West* (Princeton, 1962), p. 114.

Al-Hamadhani had as a follower a philologist and artistic writer from Basrah named abu-Muhammad al-Qasim al-Hariri (1054–1122). Al-Hariri was less original but more felicitous in expression and richer in vocabulary than his predecessor. It was he who gave the maqamah its classic form.

For one of his maqamahs he set the scene in Kufah, a leading center of Arab learning. A band of scholars are shown spending the evening together. A stranger knocks at the door. As he is admitted he recites verses of his composition describing his condition as a destitute beggar. Moved by his story and impressed by the beauty and delicacy of his poetry, the company receives him with a warm welcome. He assures his hosts that he is of royal descent and has just found a long-lost son whom he cannot support. Money is collected for him. As it is handed to him, he departs, laughingly disclosing that he had entirely fabricated the story to earn his living.

The following is the way al-Hariri introduces his maqamah:

> Related to me al-Harith ibn-Hammam [fictitious narrator of all the maqamahs]; he said: "I spent at Kufah an evening whose complexion was of double color and whose moon was a charm amulet of silver. For company I had men so nurtured on the milk of eloquence that they could throw Sahban [a proverbially eloquent orator of early Islam] into the realm of obliviousness. Each one of them had things to teach and nothing to impeach; each was one to whom a friend would incline and never decline. The night conversation was so fascinating that it was continued till moonlight cessation and sleeplessness' discontinuation.
> Now when night's unmixed darkness had thrown its shadow on us, and there was nought but nodding amongst us, a faint outside noise was heard, followed by a dog's bark and a door's knock. This made us ask, who comes in the dark? . . .[8]

For a thousand years the stylistic elegance of the maqamah did not cease to entice writers throughout the Arab world. In the mid-nineteenth century a Christian Lebanese, Nasif al-Yaziji, made a successful attempt at it. A thirteenth-century bishop in north Syria imitated the maqamah in religious Syriac compositions. Shortly before him a Spanish Jew, not satisfied with translating al-Hariri's *Maqamat*, imitated them

[8] Al-Hariri, *Maqamat*, ed. 'Isa Saba (Beirut, 1958), p. 40. Cf. Hitti, *Islam and the West*, pp. 133 et seq.; also cf. Thomas Chenery, *The Assemblies of al Hariri* (London, 1867), pp. 127 et seq. (where the entire maqamah is given).

in Hebrew. Picaresque tales, originating in sixteenth-century Spain and featuring the rogue as hero, betray an affinity to an Arabic original. So do some stories by the famed Spanish dramatist Cervantes (d. 1616), who for five years was held captive by Arabs.

The *Alf Laylah* (*Arabian Nights*) had a Persian source in *Hazar Afsana* ("thousand tales"), which was of Indian origin. As time went on, however, the *Nights* acquired new material from varied sources — Greek, Jewish, Syriac, Egyptian, and Turkish. Along with stories about Solomon, Alexander the Great, and Chosroes appeared humorous anecdotes and romances set in Harun al-Rashid's court. But the fairy tales remained the most striking part. Originally independent, the stories were brought within one framework. Their heterogeneous character inspired the modern critical remark that the *Arabian Nights* are Persian tales told after the manner of Buddha by Queen Esther to Harun al-Rashid in Cairo during the fourteenth Christian century. Though extravagant in imagery and rich in human interest, the *Nights* was never raised by the Arabs to the rank of polite literature. Its place was in the coffee house where the stories were told by professionals to amuse and entertain.

Not only are the separate stories absorbing, the framework they are placed in is distinctive. An Indian king, Shahriyar, discovers the unfaithfulness of his first wife. He then resolves to marry many others and kill them the day after the wedding. A vizir's daughter, Shahrazad, offers her services and tells him tales that hold his interest in such suspense that he spares her life to hear the last in the series. By then his anger has cooled and he makes her his queen.

Sporadically Arabian and other Eastern stories found their way early into Europe, mostly carried orally by pilgrims, other travelers, Crusaders, and merchants, giving Europeans a foretaste of the influence that was to follow. Chaucer's "Squiere's Tale" was of Arabian origin and so were some stories in the *Decameron* by Boccaccio (d. 1375), father of Italian classic prose. But the collection itself did not reach the West until later. The French version by Jean Antoine Galland (12 vols., 1704–17) was the first translation (actually it was an adaptation). In English, Edward William Lane's partial translation (3 vols., 1839–45) was followed by John Payne's (9 vols., 1882–4). Richard Burton's (10 vols., 1885–8) depended on Payne's — which was considered the best — and, in fact, often copied it.

Exotic in setting and rich in color and fantasy, these and other Eastern tales caught the fancy of European writers and readers. Reprints, modifications, and imitations in the form of Turkish tales, Persian tales, and Oriental tales mushroomed. Without them *Gulliver's Travels* and the like might not have been written. Through the *Arabian Nights* words and phrases like "afreet" (afrit, *'afrit*), "jinnee" (*jinn*), and "open sesame" became domesticated in the English language; and such stories as "Sinbad [Sindbad] the Sailor," "Aladdin ['Ala'-al-Din] and the Magic Lamp," and "Ali ['Ali] Baba and the Forty Thieves," became a part of the repertoire of almost every English-speaking child. They testify to the debt English literature owes Arabic. Not only scientific and philosophic Arab contributions but also artistic ones transcended cultural and national barriers.

The fact remains, however, that Arabs in their long history produced no truly great dramatist — no Racine, to say nothing of a Dante or a Shakespeare. At their best Arab poets had a limited horizon. The particular rather than the general interested them. Their main concern was themselves or their immediate environment. Their dealings with the world within shut them off from the world without. Nor did the Arabs produce an epic poet comparable to the Persian Firdawsi or the Greek Homer. On the mechanical side certain poetical restrictions, such as the monorhymed form, served as a deterrent to lengthy composition. Only a few poems with more than a hundred verses are known to have been written. But even more important, the necessary background of a national life rich in heroic deeds was lacking. The background of their early heroic period was tribal and that of the Islamic period was fragmented nationalism with highly religious overtones. Neither Islam the religion nor Islam the state or culture succeeded in giving the Moslem society a solid nationalistic basis.

ART

❖ IN ART as in science and philosophy the Moslem Arabian had little heritage from which to draw. Of the products of creative imagination only poetry figured prominently in pre-Islamic Hijaz. Any relics of architecture, sculpture, or painting that survived in fact or in literature were devoid of aesthetic value and could hardly qualify as pieces of art. In none of these three fields was an artistic height attained before Muhammad. None became a scholarly discipline until one or two centuries later. The same could be said about music. If Arabic provided the spiritual complex, the conquered lands to the north offered the technical knowledge and the material texture. Religion, however, remained throughout a vital force.

I

ARCHITECTURE, one of the first and most permanent of the fine arts, is associated in Islam with palaces and places of worship. As such it is well represented in South Arabia, whose culture preceded that of the North. In Hijaz the tent was the ordinary dwelling, the open air the temple, and the desert sands the tomb. Hijaz lacked royalty but not a deity. Its national shrine at Mecca was a primitive, roofless, cube-like structure, from which comes the name Kaabah ("cube"). The earliest description of the Kaabah showed that it was, in Muhammad's time, "the height of a man," with a threshold so low that heavy rains would flood the structure. Destroyed by a fire caused by a woman burning incense, the building was rebuilt by a Christian who alternated layers of wood, from a ship wrecked at Jiddah, and stone. The style of construction suggests Abyssinian origin. Youthful Muhammad, it is said, was given the honor of setting in its corner the Black Stone, to which the building evidently owed its sanctity. However, it was not the mosque that arose around the Kaabah but the mosque of the Prophet in Medina that became the prototype for religious buildings in Islam.

The Prophet's Mosque was a bare structure with no architectural pretensions. It began as a quadrangular courtyard open to the sky. It was later partly roofed, as a protection against the sun, by palm branches covered with mud and supported by trunks of palm trees, some of which had once grown on the site. The cover was an extension of a neighboring roof. A palm stump served as a stand for Muhammad to use while addressing the congregation. The stand was replaced, at the suggestion of someone who had seen a pulpit (*minbar*) in a Christian church, by a small platform of tamarisk wood. When delivering his last sermon in Mecca, the Prophet sat on his camel's back.

The worshipers arranged themselves in parallel rows facing north, toward Jerusalem. In 624 when the revelation came to change the direction (*qiblah*) while Muhammad was in the midst of prayer, all he did was to turn south to face Mecca. No indicator of direction (*mihrab*) seemed necessary, nor was the need felt for a special structure for the caller to prayer (*mu'adhdhin*, muezzin). The first muezzin was an Abyssinian ex-slave named Bilal who at the proper moment would climb to the flat roof of the adjacent building and attract by his stentorian voice all believers. This simple Medinese structure had in embryo all the essential features of the future congregational mosque: sheltered courtyard, pulpit, qiblah, and minaret.

Those generals who established lasting military camps, such as those at Kufah and Basrah which developed into leading centers of cultured Islam, were mostly Companions of the Prophet and had, no doubt, worshiped with him in the Medinese mosque. In building mosques for their camps they had no model to follow other than the one in Medina. But as cities were later occupied and used as capitals the situation radically changed. The mosque, as it were, stepped into the shell of the church. Damascus offered a conspicuous example.

When the provincial Byzantine capital was occupied, it had an elaborate cathedral dedicated to Saint John the Baptist. The cathedral built by Emperor Theodosius (d. 395) on the site of an earlier Roman temple of Jupiter was now divided and shared as a place of worship by Moslems and Christians. In 705 Caliph al-Walid took over the entire building and rebuilt it as the grand Umayyad Mosque, which then became — as it still is — the fourth sanctuary in Eastern Islam after those in Mecca, Medina, and Jerusalem. The "burial place" of the head of Saint John (Yahya) is still shown in the mosque. In its construction and decoration the caliph employed Syrian, Byzantine, Egyptian, and Persian craftsmen and artists who turned out a work in keeping with the dignity and prestige of the new empire. The walls were sumptuously decorated with mosaics of gold and precious stones, according to a tenth-century geographer, and bore representations of trees and other beautiful objects. Covered later by a conservative caliph, the ornamentation was rediscovered in 1928. This mosque served as a model for mosques from Syria through North Africa to Spain. In fact the entire Damascus mosque became the accepted form for Islamic religious buildings. It is the earliest mosque to have survived practically intact with its rich decoration in colored marble and polychrome mosaic.

In particular, two of the features of the original cathedral were adapted for Islam and have been perpetuated in all mosques until the present day. These were the minarets and the niche in the wall to indicate the proper direction of prayer. Two of the minarets which al-Walid kept for his place of worship had been the church towers of the basilica; the third — on the north side — had evidently been a beacon tower. The word "minaret," it should be recalled, means "light" or "fire place." The church towers must have originated as watchtowers or places for signaling at night by fire. An Arab geographer, ibn-al-Faqih, one of the earliest to describe the building, states that one of the minarets was a watchtower of the church and was left by al-Walid.

The mihrab, which is generally recessed and horseshoe-shaped, is clearly derived from the apse behind the church altar. Altars were at that time oriented eastward and the apse was usually semicircular. It was easily adapted for Moslem use, for once the east is determined, the south becomes easy to find. As they developed, the pulpit and the mihrab became the recipients of the artist's special care. Their multicolor decoration in floral, mosaic, geometrical, and calligraphic designs represents a triumph of Islamic art.

Earlier and more artistic but architecturally less influential was the Dome of the Rock (Qubbat al-Sakhrah) of Jerusalem, built in 691 by al-Walid's father 'Abd-al-Malik. The site is traditionally the one on which Caliph 'Umar in 638 built a simple place of worship; thus the name "Mosque of 'Umar" is sometimes wrongly applied to the present one. The site also marks the place where Solomon's Temple, a Roman temple, and a church once stood. This makes it one of the most sacred spots on earth.

The caliph's intent was to produce a structure that would outshine the nearby Church of the Holy Sepulcher and rival the one then in the hands of an enemy. Paying no heed to the architectural design of the old mosque, the caliph worked out a plan featuring a domed rotunda, clearly inspired by the Christian church. Some of the material on the old site was no doubt used. Imitations and variations of the domed mosque appeared throughout the world, its finest examples appearing in Constantinople during the Ottoman reign, when church architecture attained a high point of development.

The dome was not the only innovation in the Qubbah. Mosaic forms, stone carvings, and other decorative motifs of Hellenistic and Persian derivation were introduced. Mosaic decoration in the East first appeared in Assyria. Obviously the caliph employed Byzantines or Byzantine-trained Syrians, as well as Persians, in the construction. The result was an architectural masterpiece of beauty that has not been equaled in the Arab world. The Turks particularly under Sulayman the Magnificent (d. 1566) with his Sulaymaniyah Mosque, the Persians under 'Abbas the Great (d. 1629) with his Isfahan mosques, and the Moslem Indians under Shah Jahan (d. 1666), builder of Taj Mahal, rivaled if not excelled the Arabs under 'Abd-al-Malik. Interestingly, an efflorescence of architectural art in Islam took place after the decay of its philosophy and science. To Moslems everywhere, however, the Dome of the Rock has remained more than a place of worship or a historical and artistic object: it has been a living symbol of their faith. That is its significance in the current Arab-Israeli conflict.

Near the Dome 'Abd-al-Malik erected (701) another distinguished structure — al-Masjid al-Aqsa ("the farther mosque"), echoing a passage in the Koran (17:1). The passage, "Glorified be He who made His servant journey by night from the Holy Mosque [of Mecca] to the farther mosque," is responsible for the story of the nocturnal journey (isra'). The site of the Aqsa was once occupied by Saint Mary's Church, which was built by Justinian and destroyed by Chosroes immediately before the Moslem conquest. The builder made use of the ruins of the church. Tradition locates Solomon's stables nearby. Demolished by an earthquake (ca. 771) the mosque was rebuilt by the 'Abbasid al-Mansur and later modified into a church by the Crusaders. Now known as "al-Haram al-Sharif" ("the noble sanctuary") it is the site of an ensemble of mosques, tombs, dervish monasteries, and public fountains, added in part by caliphs and sultans down to Sulayman the Magnificent. It ranks in sanctity next to the sacred mosques of Mecca and Medina.

On its journey east to China and west to Spain, the mosque picked up local elements which did not change its basic plan. As a place of worship, it remained generally simple and dignified, derived from earlier patterns but singularly expressive of the new faith. In its evolution it epitomized the history of the development of Moslem culture — of which it was an expression — in its international and interracial relationships. It tangibly illustrates the interplay between Islam and its neighbors. To the spiritually sensitive believer, however, evolution is of no concern. As he enters the open-to-the-sky courtyard, circumscribed by aisles, he is disposed to feel detachment from surroundings and a simultaneous uplift heavenward. The tall, slender minaret seems like a finger pointing upward. Inside the main structure, the vault with its resplendent lamps looks like a replica of the celestial dome. The ornamented mihrab directs his attention to the source of his faith. The seemingly endless rows of columns suggest infinity. Other worshipers around generate the feeling of membership in a worldwide fraternity.

THE Umayyad contribution to architecture was not limited to the religious field. The caliphs of Damascus were the first to build royal palaces (those of Medina lived in mud huts as the Prophet did). Strangely, the palaces they built were not in the capital but on the fringe of the Syrian desert. They were intended as bath halls and pleasure houses for relaxing, playing, and satisfying the Arab's nostalgic feeling for the desert. While at these retreats caliphs and princes engaged in hunting, drinking, bathing, and watching dancing girls. What makes the buildings remarkable is not only that they introduced artistic secular architecture but that they were the medium through which representational art was introduced into Islam. The remains of these palaces are strewn along the western fringe of the desert, often where Roman fortresses once stood.

The best known palace is that of the great builder al-Walid. Its name, "Qusayr ["palacette"] 'Amrah," sounds modern; there is no trace of it in Arabic literature. The palace lies east of the Jordan River in a direct line from the northern edge of the Dead Sea. It is known for its murals which include portraits of six royal personages, one of whom is presumably Chosroes, and another Roderick, the Visigothic king of Spain overthrown by the Umayyads about the time this palace was built. The theme is clearly the glorification of the Moslem dynasty. The symbolic figures represent Victory, Philosophy, History, and Poetry. Certain names appear over the pictures in Greek, others in Arabic. There are also representations of nude dancers, musicians, and merrymakers. A hunting scene depicts a lion attacking a wild ass. The ornamentation comprises fruit-bearing palm trees and laurels, foliage growing out of vases, and birds of the desert. These extraordinary mural paintings are undoubtedly the product of Syrian and Persian craftsmen. They represent the passage of Byzantine iconography and technique into the Islamic culture.

Larger, better preserved, and more striking is Khirbat ("ruins of") al-Mafjar, built by al-Walid's brother and successor Hisham (724–43). Hisham was the grandfather of 'Abd-al-Rahman I, founder of the Umayyad dynasty in Spain. The palace lies four miles north of Jericho. The recently excavated remains indicate there was an open court surrounded by arcades and equipped with a mosque and a richly decorated bath hall. The gate is decorated with figural sculptures, one of which is presumed to be a representation of the caliph himself. The floors of the audience room and the bath hall are covered with mosaics which display a variety of geometric patterns. The ceiling of the hall leading to the bathroom is decorated with carved and molded plaster in the forms of acanthus rosettes and grapevines. The style of the human heads around the central rosette recalls stucco sculpture found in central Asia.

The architectural art, developed in eighth-century Syria, reached its highest form in the thirteenth- and fourteenth-century citadel-palace of Alhambra in Granada. The succession of courts and halls with their rich and delicate decoration — painted and gilded — have not ceased to charm visitors from all over the world.

The majority of buildings are grouped around the Court of Lions — named for the stone figures on which the basin of a fountain rests. Sumptuously decorated arcades, molded of plaster, stand on alternating single and double marble columns of unusual grace and lightness. Through the interaction and repetition of motifs and designs the entire court becomes, in the words of an authority, "a rare symphony of decoration."

Of the many halls in the Alhambra, the Hall of Ambassadors is especially striking in architecture and ornamentation. Huge in size and square in form, it is crowned with a vast dome that has no middle support but rests directly on the walls. The ceiling is luxuriously ornamented and painted. Other halls in the complex were not neglected by the artist, but this one, the reception hall for distinguished guests, received his special attention.

Throughout, the epigraphic and the floral designs form the general base of the decorations. The prevailing colors are red and blue. The calligraphic and foliage motifs are set in geometric networks to compose the faïence. The inscriptions include verses of original poetry as well as pious sayings, forming at times interlacing bands. Colors, foliage, and lettering cooperate to render Alhambra the supreme example of Arab decoration not only in the West but throughout the world.

162

UNLIKE architecture, painting and sculpture and music encountered, in varying degrees, difficulties in Islam with religious strictures, justified and unjustified. History hardly remembers the name of an Arab painter and evidently never knew an Arab sculptor, although it has preserved the names of many musicians. The situation is now changing rapidly under the impact of the West, and names of modern artists-sculptors as well as musicians are widely publicized.

In early times, in all countries, man endowed the products of representational art — whether painted or sculptured — with magical properties. For him the representation of an object stood for the object itself. Thus the ancient Egyptians, who were the first to entertain a clear idea of life after death, buried with their dead not only food but sometimes pictures of it instead on the assumption that failing the substance, its representation would do.

Early Arabians worshiped idols. These were images or representations in stone, wood, or metal. One of them, the Black Stone of Mecca, has survived. The Baghdadi author ibn-al-Kalbi (d. 819) wrote a volume entitled *Kitab al-Asnam* ("the book of idols"). The Koran mentions by name seven idols of Hijaz, including three females (Allat, Manah, and al-'Uzza), daughters of Allah, although Hubal, the probable head deity of the Kaabah, is not mentioned. Muhammad's biography adds that on his victorious entry into Mecca in 630, he went around the Kaabah touching with his spear the three hundred and sixty idols, each of which immediately fell to the ground. The pictures of the prophets on the walls of the sanctuary he ordered erased by washing with water from the Zamzam. Only one picture was spared, that of Jesus and Mary, which Muhammad had covered with his hands.

The Hebrews were the first people to develop an abstract concept of the deity and the first to forbid his representation. How much influence that precedent exercised on Islam is hard to ascertain. Certain hadiths sound similar to Hebrew traditions: both agree that the interdiction of images relates to animate beings (men and animals) and not to plants and inanimate objects; the Old Testament idea that God created man in his image also found its way into a hadith. But the Moslem theologians' opposition to the art of representation did have a koranic basis.

The basis is semantic. The Koran uses the word for "creating" synonymously with the word for "forming," "fashioning," or "making an image." "He it is who formeth you in the wombs, as pleaseth Him. There is no god but He, the sublime, the wise" (3:4). "We created you and formed you, then We said to the angels, 'fall ye prostrate before Adam'" (7:10). "He is Allah, the Creator, the Maker, the Former. His are the beautiful names" (59:24). The verb "form" (*sawwar*) and its derivative "former" (*musawwir*) are precisely the words used for drawing a picture or making an image and for painter or sculptor. The ulama then argued that the representation of men and animals was the prerogative of God and God alone, and any intruder is a blasphemer. The Prophet reportedly declared that those to be most severely punished on the day of judgment would be the *musawwirs*, imitators of Allah's work. This hadith based on the Prophet's words was supported by another involving his action. When one day Muhammad opened the door and saw a cushion with pictures which 'A'ishah had just purchased, he refused to enter the house on the ground that angels do not enter a home containing images. The uncompromising attitude of the Koran toward monotheism and its insistent prohibition of idolatry must have lent credence to such hadiths.

The prejudicial attitude of legists toward plastic as well as pictorial art did not crystallize until the second century, but even then their hostility was at times as ineffective as the koranic prohibition of wine. As the Moslem aristocracy indulged in the luxurious living of the Near East society, they developed a taste for the beautiful and yielded to the temptation of utilizing the experience and artistic skill of their subjects. Al-Mansur set up the figure of a horseman on the green dome of his palace in his newly built capital. 'Abd-al-Rahman III had the statue of his favorite wife, al-Zahra', installed atop the palace named after her. A governor of Egypt (Khumarawayh, 884–95) adorned his residence with life-size wooden statues of himself and his wives wearing gold crowns. But nowhere do we find in a mosque a representation of a man or an animal. Painting and sculpture, therefore, were not pressed into the service of religion and did not become its handmaidens as they did in Buddhism and Christianity. They — especially painting — became secular arts and were patronized by princes and aristocrats.

Creative activity in painting was channeled mainly into miniature painting and decorating household goods. Miniature painting lent itself particularly to illustrating books. Two principal schools evolved — one in Persia, revealing Chinese influence in the facial features, and one in Syria-Iraq, which arose under Christian influence. The earliest illustrated Arabic manuscript extant is a miniature astronomical work of the early eleventh century. In the two following centuries *Kalilah wa-Dimnah* and al-Hariri's *Maqamat* (both discussed in the preceding chapter) were enriched with miniature paintings in color and included representations of men and animals. A comparison with Jacobite and Nestorian prayerbook illustrations betrays close affinity in style. Since the early Moslem had scruples against human representation, they first utilized the talents of the conquered people. Persia was particularly fertile in the early production of Moslem painters of miniatures, an art form in which Islam made a distinctive contribution. In painting as in architecture, the subject peoples were the purveyors of Islamic art.

Art as applied to decorating household goods was a luxury; only the well-to-do could afford it. In this art, also, Moslems developed further what had been early, venerable traditions of metalwork, glassware, ceramics, and fabrics. Centuries before Islam, the Persians were masters of decorative design and color. With the rise of Islam they were able to influence their Arab neighbors and cooperate with them to raise the minor arts to a degree of excellence unattained before. In the medieval era Moslem ceramics reached a new height in beauty of decoration. In lustered pottery, where designs are painted on a glazed surface and fixed by firing to produce a metallic gleam, Moslem artists achieved one of their triumphs. Their motifs were mainly floral, geometric, epigraphic, and at times figural. Tiles were introduced by Persians into Damascus and were used together with mosaics for interior and exterior decoration. Their use spread throughout the Middle East. In such Phoenician towns as Tyre and Sidon, where colored glass originated, the processes of enameling and gilding were almost perfected.

Examples of the most splendid achievements of Syrian glassworkers are mosque lamps, ornamented with medallions, inscriptions, and floral patterning and — following the Christian model — suspended by chains from the ceiling.

Carpet-weaving, begun in Pharaonic Egypt, continued to develop under Islam, acquiring new motifs and coloring. Hunting and garden scenes were favored. Not only in Egypt but in Persia and the entire Fertile Crescent, the textile art was well developed before the advent of the Arabians. Decorated silk fabrics, the product of handlooms in Syria, were introduced by Crusaders, pilgrims, and travelers into Europe, where they were later imitated. Museums of art in the East and West display objects from 'Abbasid Iraq and from Fatimid and Mamluk Egypt and Syria that catch the eyes of streams of visitors. The objects include carpets and textiles; vases, ewers, and incense burners shaped as or decorated with birds and other animals; ceramic lamps, plates, and bowls painted with brilliant, radiant lusters and acquiring through the centuries metallic glazes of changing rainbow hues.

Moslem artists made significant contributions not only in lustering but in improved techniques of glazing. It is interesting to note that whereas in science and philosophy the Moslems reached their peak of achievement early and then made no more progress, this was not true in art. The creative glow was not dimmed until the mid-seventeenth century. The continuators of the tradition, however, were not Arabs, but Turks — Ottoman and Saljuk — and Mongols.

IV

ISLAMIC art has been rightly called a decorative art; this is especially true of its Arab variety. The Arab artist, like the Arab poet, depended for effectiveness primarily on style and form. His main values were decorative. His aim was the creation of a pleasing if not exciting combination of form and color. He, again like the poet, did not mind repetition. In fact repetition may be said to have been his favorite technique. In art as in poetry the Arab displayed keen appreciation for the particular, the individual, but not for the whole of which that particular was but a fragment. In one respect, however, Arab art differed from Arab poetry: it had no indigenous origin.

166

The style of ornamentation thus developed by the Moslem Arab became known to Westerners as "arabesque." In general arabesque is lacking in content and in symbolic value. Its use on buildings, textiles, ceramics, metalwork, glassware, and books is purely ornamental. Starting in the eighth century under the Umayyads, it picked up Hellenistic and Persian (Sasanid) elements, and acquired its typical form under the 'Abbasids. This type of decoration spread over the entire Moslem area, including Spain. The distinctive elements of arabesque, as noted above, are floral or vegetal, geometric, and epigraphic or calligraphic. The three are stylized, harmonized, and set in patterns. The figural element is not always lacking. The figures may represent hunting, banquet, or game scenes, usually medallion-shaped.

The vegetal elements used are acanthus, vine leaves, and trefoil; the favorite flowers are tulips, roses, and almond blossoms, all denaturalized and conventionalized, with no pretension to reality. The classical derivation is here unmistakable: in this respect the arabesque can be said to have continued the Hellenistic foliage tradition. This, however, cannot be said of the second decorative element, the geometric. The geometric figures are abstractions. Even more original is the lettering used decoratively. Arabic letters lend themselves admirably to such purposes and may have no parallel except in Chinese characters. In no other art did calligraphy play such a conspicuous role.

Arabesque composition is expressed by the interlacing of patterns with a rhythmic alternating movement. Abstract geometrical designs are used in an infinite pattern. Geometrically combined bands are similarly combined with foliage. Geometric, vegetal, and calligraphic designs are joined into endless variations on a few themes. The regulating principle is reciprocal repetition. In the arabesque scheme Arabic writing is the only element with more than decorative value. As the decoration lures the viewer and the endless abstractions carry him away, he may at last come to the only tangible thing. The bands of inscriptions quote koranic or poetic compositions and repeat pious sayings and the names of Allah. Christianity dramatized its story by human imagery, a procedure Islam could not follow because of religious prejudice; hence the arabesque.

Arabesque left a rich legacy in Spain and through Spain in Europe, where it became known as "moresque" (from Moor, originally "a native of Morocco"). Spanish vessels were decorated with pseudo-Arabic inscriptions and Christian heraldic devices. In Sicily meaningless imitations of Arabic script were used even before they were in Spain. Various kinds of colored tiles, still favorites in Spain and Portugal, bear their Arabic name *azulejo* (*al-zulayji*). Caskets and boxes of ivory, decorated with carved, inlaid, or painted ornaments, were used as jewel cases and perfume boxes. Oriental silk textiles, with their rich coloring and floral and geometric designs were in demand for aristocratic robes, church investments, and wrappings for relics of saints. France and Italy followed Spain and Sicily, and during the period of the Renaissance, arabesque was in wide use throughout Europe.

Aside from its use in arabesque, calligraphy can claim the right of being an art by itself. Its prestige came from its use to perpetuate the word of God and it enjoyed the approval of the Koran (68:1; 96:4). Thus, Arabic writing developed into a highly prized art. Surah 68 is dedicated to the pen (*qalam*) and commentators on it assert that the implement used in writing is a divine gift, the first thing created by God. Koran copyists through the ages vied with one another to excel not only in accuracy but in the elegance of their handwriting. If accuracy was pleasing unto Allah, elegance was pleasing to the wealthy buyer.

The earliest form of Arabic lettering, called "Kufic" (from Kufah), was angular in shape and favored for koranic usage over a period of some five centuries. The ordinary cursive script, called "Naskhi" (from a root word meaning "to copy"), has now practically replaced the older form. Both lend themselves to decorative purposes. Arabic literature has honorably preserved the names of calligraphers beginning with the days of al-Ma'mun, a fact which contrasts sharply with the omission of names of painters and other artists. Of all artistic fields, calligraphy is the only one in which moderns surpass their predecessors. The pre-Kemalist Turks produced the finest calligraphers, specializing in official documents.

V

MUSIC, in the sense of organized sound with an element of rhythm, must have existed in Arabia from earliest times. Arabians no doubt shared with other ancient Semites some theory and practice of music about which little is known. Pre-Muhammadan Hijaz was exposed to cultural influences, including music, from the petty Arab kingdoms of Hirah and Ghassan respectively on the Persian and the Syro-Byzantine borders.

Wine, women, and song were the three pleasures dearest to the Bedouin heart. To the urban settler in Hijaz, music and song were an essential feature of social as well as religious life. The fairs in 'Ukaz and the pilgrimages to the Kaabah were celebrated with song and music. Before the revelation, Muhammad must have witnessed if not participated in such ceremonies. The caravan had its special chants, which cameleers used to mitigate the toils of the journey. Then, too, there were professional singers, mostly women and slave-girls. The women who at Badr and Uhud sang battle songs to fire the enthusiasm of the Moslem warriors were following an early precedent.

Controversy swirled around attempts to determine Muhammad's precise attitude toward music. In his zeal to alienate his followers from polytheism, he reacted against practices associated with it. Anything that smacked of idolatry was anathema to him. The vehement koranic denunciation of poetry is an illustration. The Arab poet as a rule was as much a musician as he was a poet. He often sang his verses or had one with a better voice sing them for him. Music and poetry were intimately associated in Muhammad's mind. The Koran, however, has not a word against music. Certain disapproving theologians thought they found some justification in the following vaguely worded passage:

> Among the people are those who buy a frivolous discourse, that they may lead astray from the path of Allah without knowledge, and make it the butt of mockery. For such there is a shameful punishment.
> When our signs are recited unto them, they turn disdainfully away as if they heard them not, as if their ears had deafness. Give them tidings of a painful punishment.
>
> (31:5–6)

Other theologians disagree on the interpretation, asserting that the reference is to Persian tales rather than musical compositions.

What the Koran missed the hadith obligingly supplied. Objectors to music found more than one hadith attributed to the Prophet by no

169

less an authority than 'A'ishah. One hadith has him say, "The musical instrument is the devil's muezzin." In due course all four orthodox schools of law, liberal and conservative (Hanafi, Maliki, Shafi'i, Hanbali), condemned not only playing music (*al-sama'*) but listening to it.

But the supposed executors of the law turned out to be its executioners. It was all started with those "ungodly usurpers," as the Umayyads were called by Shi'ite and 'Abbasid authors, and particularly by the second caliph, Yazid (680–83), son of a Christian mother. It was Yazid who introduced players and singers — male and female, free and slave — into the caliphal court, where they became a fixture. The trend started by him intensified under his late successors, one of whom considered "lending ear" to music the only true pleasure in life.

Early in the 'Abbasid period the liberal Persian attitude toward music began to jell. Certain conservative and pious caliphs tried to enforce the ban on music in their courts but the current gradually assumed flood proportions, reaching lower courts and aristocratic establishments, and no dam could stand in its way. "The law against 'listening to music' has been honoured more in the breach than in the observance." [1]

In the galaxy that illumined the courts of Harun al-Rashid and his sons al-Amin and al-Ma'mun were many musical stars. The virtuosi among them were more than mere musicians. They were composers of song and poetry and at times scholars versed in the sciences of the day, with memories stocked with choice verses and delightful anecdotes. The stock of his anecdotes and his capacity for wine determined a musician's usefulness as a caliph's boon companion. Below the virtuosi stood the instrumentalists, mostly lutanists. Viol performers were considered inferior. Among the female singers were artistes bought at high prices and included as ornaments in the caliphal harem. Some of these songstresses were extremely talented and they could repeat thousands of poems and songs. Such male and female masters of music and song, thriving in the Baghdad court during its heyday, have furnished the theme for a number of fantastic anecdotes. These stories are held in perpetuity on the pages of the *Arabian Nights* and of specialized history works such as *Kitab al-Aghani* ("book of songs," 21 vols.),

[1] Henry G. Farmer, *A History of Arabian Music* (London, 1929), p. 31.

170

written by al-Isfahani in the mid-tenth century, and *al-'Iqd al-Farid* ("the unique necklace," 4 vols.) by his contemporary ibn-'Abd-Rabbihi. According to a story, two thousand musicians and singers once took part in a performance given under Harun's patronage. In a similar soiree given by al-Amin only one thousand participated, but the caliph made up for this by keeping the party, including his family, singing and dancing till dawn.

More names of musicians and singers have been recorded in Arabian history than in any other field of art with the exception of poetry. Two names stand out — those of Ibrahim al-Mawsili and his son Ishaq. Ibrahim, the patriarch of Arab music, was born (742) in Mosul of Persian parentage. When he was young he was kidnapped and in his captivity learned brigand songs. Arabic tradition credits him with being the first to beat the rhythm with a wand. So sensitive was his ear to music that he could spot a girl with an ill-tuned instrument among thirty lute-players. When Harun took him as a cup companion he offhandedly bestowed on him one hundred fifty thousand dirhams and assigned to him ten thousand dirhams a month. For a single song the caliph once rewarded him with one hundred thousand dirhams. Ibrahim died in Baghdad in 804.

His son and pupil Ishaq (767–850) inherited his talent and in due course exceeded his father's accomplishments. As dean of the musicians of the age, Ishaq in his career personified the spirit of classical Arabic music. He was to al-Ma'mun and al-Mutawakkil what his father had been to their ancestors, a musician and a companion. More learned than his rivals and predecessors, Ishaq qualified as a poet, philologist, and juriconsult and owned one of the richest private libraries in the capital. His students were in great demand. For a female slave student of his a messenger of Egypt's governor offered thirty thousand dinars, a sum matched by an envoy of the Byzantine emperor and increased to forty thousand by a representative of the ruler of Khurasan. Ishaq solved the problem by freeing the girl and taking her for his wife. The tribute his patron al-Mutawakkil paid him shows the esteem in which he was held: "In the death of Ishaq my realm was deprived of an ornament and a glory."

It was during this time that the Greek musical tradition became a

171

part of Islamic culture through translations of Greek works. Music, it will be recalled, was considered a branch of philosophy and was therefore discussed in Aristotle's works. Thus the systems of Greek and Arabic music did not look radically different. Whatever was imported from the Greeks did not supersede the native system but served to enrich it. It was then that the word *musiqi* (*musiqa*) entered Arabic. The Arabs had a generic term (*ghina'*) for both song and music.

Translation served as a prelude to origination. The originators in this field were the philosophers (studied in chapter 8) headed by al-Kindi (801–ca. 873), who served in al-Ma'mun's court. Al-Kindi was the first great theorist of music in Arabic. He was a master of both systems and a contributor to his native one. He added a theoretic fifth string to the lute, reaching thereby the double octave without resorting to the shift. By using alphabetic notation for one octave he went beyond Greek musicians. As a physician al-Kindi must have had some realization of the therapeutic value of music, for — according to a story — with it he treated and cured a paralyzed boy whom all orthodox physicians in Baghdad had failed to help. Of his fifteen treatises on music — in the title of one of which "musiqi" is used probably for the first time — only five have survived.

The precedent established by this philosopher-musician was followed by his coreligionist intellectuals. They all treated music as a branch of mathematics, itself considered a philosophical discipline. The most distinguished among them in music was al-Farabi (870–950), of Turkish parentage. Al-Farabi excelled in both theory and performance. He flourished in the brilliant court of Sayf-al-Dawlah al-Hamdani of Aleppo, a replica in miniature of Harun's court. In the presence of his patron, Arab sources assure us, al-Farabi could play the lute so as to make the audience burst into laughter, shed tears, or fall asleep. Tradition claims he invented the *rabab* (rebec, viol) and the *qanun* (kanoon), though probably he only improved them. From his pen came five books on music, one of which — *Kitab al-Musiqi al-Kabir* ("the major book on music") — is the most important work on the theory of Arabic music. In Farmer's opinion, "His treatment of the physical and physiological principles of sound in music is certainly an advance on the Greeks." [2] Al-Farabi practiced Sufism and some of his compositions are still chanted in Sufi ritual.

The last great exponent of philosophy in the East, ibn-Sina (Avicenna, d. 1037), was likewise the last exponent of the theory of music. This physician and philosopher included in his works on philosophy, particularly *al-Shifa'* and *al-Najah*, long chapters on music. His contribution lay in the detailed description of the instruments then used and in the treatment of points in Greek musical theory that have since been lost. This philosopher like his predecessor was interested in Sufism, but he did not practice it.

Sufism was responsible for endowing music with respectability. To Sufis, music was a means to achieve the emotional, ecstatic state that preceded revelation. An early ascetic, the celebrated Egyptian dhu-al-Nun (d. 860), drew a fine distinction in combating the legists' arguments against music. "Listening to music has a divine effect that moves the heart to Allah. He who listens to it spiritually attains to Him, but he who listens sensually falls into heresy." But the chief credit should go to that great intellectual theologian al-Ghazzali (d. 1111) for his convincing arguments in favor of this form of art. In his discussion of music and ecstasy (*al-sama' w-al-wajd*) he presented six reasons for considering singing a more potent force in producing ecstasy than reciting the Koran. Not only did al-Ghazzali allow song and music but dancing, too, saying that all were means of intensifying religious feeling. He, however, made certain reservations, chief of which was that the performers should be male. Thanks to al-Ghazzali's and others' efforts music established itself as a feature in Sufi ritual.

The Arab philosophical tradition of the East passed into the Moslem West without its musical component. The first Moslem philosopher in Spain, ibn-Masarrah (d. 931), showed no interest in music, nor did the last and greatest, ibn-Rushd (d. 1198). Ibn-Rushd did paraphrase Aristotle's *Poetics* and *Rhetoric*, but he cannot be said to have himself made a contribution. The only exception might be the physician-philosopher ibn-Bajjah (Avenpace, d. 1138), but none of his works have survived.

[2] *The Encyclopaedia of Islam* (Leiden, 1936), vol. 3, p. 751.

In the practice of music, however, the case is different. The founder of the Andalusian school was a tenor of Persian origin named Ziryab (d. ca. 860). Ziryab received his education under the two Mawsili masters in Baghdad but migrated to North Africa when he aroused the jealousy of Ishaq. While there he was invited to Cordova by 'Abd-al-Rahman II (822–52), a ruler who dreamed of making of his capital another Baghdad. The monarch rode out in person to welcome his guest. The newcomer was feted and then established in baronial style at an estate valued at forty thousand dinars. The annuity assigned amounted to 5640 dinars. In the tradition of his two masters, Ziryab was a poet, a belletrist, a wit, and a student of science, specifically astronomy and geography. He reportedly knew by heart the words and tunes of ten thousand songs. Like Ibrahim and Ishaq he claimed to have learned many wonderful melodies while he slept. He was one of four persons who exercised the largest measure of influence on 'Abd-al-Rahman, the other three being the monarch's wife, his vizir, and his eunuch chamberlain. The musician's intimacy with 'Abd-al-Rahman and the huge bounties he received became subjects of public criticism.

More enduring, however, was the artistic influence this master musician exercised. He is credited with adding a fifth string to the lute (evidently in the West) and substituting for the wooden plectrum one made of eagles' talons. His conservatory in Cordova attracted students from a wide area and established the tradition of Arabic Spanish music. Its influence reached beyond Spain into northwestern Africa.

An idea of the impression which Arabic music in general left on the West may be gained by reviewing the names of some instruments borrowed by Spanish or other European languages. Besides Spain, Sicily and Syria under the Crusaders served as bridges for transmitting Arab culture. One of the best known instruments thus transmitted was the lute (from Ar. *al-'ud,* "a piece of wood"). The 'ud, evidently developed in Arab Hirah, made its way into Hijaz less than a century before Muhammad, accompanied the Moslems on the triumphal march through North Africa, and finally crossed over into Spain and Sicily to cover the Continent. Among other instruments there were the rebec (rebeck, ribibe, from Ar. *rabab*), guitar (*qitar*), timbal (*tabl*), kanoon (canun, *qanun*), and naker (kettledrum, *naqqarah*). In music as in other arts, in sciences, and in philosophy Arab contributions to Western culture were considerable. It could be said that what the Arabs borrowed from the ancient Europeans they returned to the medieval Europeans — with interest.

CONFRONTATION WITH MODERNITY

❖ THE fall of the Moslem caliphate in the mid-thirteenth century, the successive Mongol invasions, and the rise of the successor states — mostly Persian and Turkish — left the Arab world in a state of blackout that lasted for no less than six centuries. It was a period of political and spiritual stagnation. The cause of the spiritual decadence, however, was not the loss of political power; the cause was internal rather than external. When a storm blows, it is the tree with the rotten core that is toppled.

Books continued to be written, but they were mostly new versions of old material or commentaries on older books. Pseudo-scientific and quasi-literary works glutted the market. The literary masterpieces by Ghazzali, Mutanabbi, Khwarizmi, and ibn-Sina were degraded by irrational and irrelevant productions. Notable exceptions were the writings of the Tunisian ibn-Khaldun (1332–1406), a pioneer in the philosophy of history and the first social scientist.

If Islam at its best raised Arab society to a new height of human progress, at its worst it reached a low point of stagnation. Attachment to the past and isolation from the Christian West severely affected the progress of Islamic culture. The concept of progress was replaced by one of self-complacency rendered more perilous by an exaggerated feeling of superiority. The measure of achievement stood in reverse proportion to this sense of superiority. Through the ages the Arabs cherished their pride in Islam, source of their greatness and glory — a feeling that at no time was shared by Turks or Persians.

The conquest of Arab lands by Ottoman Turks in the early sixteenth century did not reverse the downward drift of Arab culture; if anything, it accelerated it. The Ottoman caliphate claimed successorship to the Arab caliphate. Its sultans assumed the traditional title of "commander of the believers." Historical distortions notwithstanding, the Ottoman regime could be considered a revival of Islam the state. Turkish became the language of the state. The caliph was no more a descendant of the Prophet's family, as required by the Sunnites, or a descendant of the Prophet himself, as required by the Shi'ites; he was not even an Arab.

All this was taking place while the West was pulling itself out of its dark ages and entering a new era of renaissance, reformation, and enlightenment leading to a revolution in science and industry. The West had embarked on a new voyage to discover fresh truths, to find rational explanations for social happenings and physical phenomena, and to establish man's increased control over his environment. In science it realized that the secret of endless knowledge lay in experimentation, and in man's affairs the secret of progress was change — change for the better. The marriage of science to man's practical needs raised technology to a height undreamed of before. The steam engine pushing forward became the symbol of the West, while the spindle remained the symbol of the East. The creative effort of Europe resulted in a new culture that was in a couple of centuries to revolutionize the cultures of the entire world. This is the modern culture. England and France were the first to modernize themselves; they were also the first to modernize the Arab East.

Modernization, then, involves the adoption of ideas, practices, and institutions developed by Western Europeans. The process presupposes responsiveness on the part of the recipient society and sufficient contact with the more developed one. These conditions prevailed in the Arab East in the nineteenth century.

I

THE invasion of Egypt by Napoleon (1798–1801) and the occupation of Algeria (1810) and Tunisia (1881) by France made clear in the Arabs' mind that their culture was no longer superior — at least not in military matters. In 1882 the British occupied Egypt, the largest and most important Arab land. At the end of World War I France was given the mandate over Lebanon and Syria, while Great Britain received the one over Palestine and Iraq. Most of these Ottoman provinces had enjoyed a high measure of autonomy: Lebanon's autonomy, for instance, had had the guarantee of the great powers since 1861. The first major confrontation between Arab Islam and modernity was then political and represented *force majeure.*

By the end of or subsequent to World War II all the Arab countries that were under the Ottomans had been liberated. They all adopted a modernized form of government, featuring parliaments, elections, and cabinets. The traditional leadership was replaced by a new one from the middle strata of society. Civil, commercial, and criminal laws based on European codes were introduced in defiance of the shari'ah. The creation of law — as was discussed in chapter 3 — was not within the province of the state. Nevertheless for centuries the Moslem communities had been circumventing their divine law by reading into it, reinterpreting it, and finally relegating it to its last refuge — the personal status, involving marriage, divorce, inheritance, and adoption of children. Today in almost all the countries here discussed any authority that the shari'ah might have is more theoretical than practical, except, of course, in Arabia proper. All modernized Arab countries, however, still pay lip service to the shari'ah, and some have included in their constitutions provisions for a Moslem head of the state. None have gone as far as Turkey, whose attack on the shari'ah was frontal rather than oblique and whose modernization, begun by Mustafa Kemal, has continued.

A Western importation closely related and also in conflict with Islam was the concept of nationalism. This dynamic concept found an enthusiastic reception in the hearts and minds of Arabs from Morocco to Iraq. It enhanced resistance to foreign domination — even if it was by Turkish Moslems — and it reinforced the urge for self-assertion and full independence. In its modern sense nationalism is a purely secular movement with geographical limits and economic values. It demands loyalty to a territorial unit that transcends all other loyalties, not excluding the religious. Islam, on the other hand, recognizes no geographical frontiers, features spiritual values, and demands supreme loyalty.

Western-style-educated Christians, mostly Lebanese, were responsible for the introduction of nationalism to the Arabic-speaking world. Their starting point was intellectual. The ideal was to unify all Arabic-speaking peoples regardless of religions on a common ground of language and culture, drawing inspiration from the glory of their past civilization and following the Western European model of government. Lebanese and Syrian journalists, writers, and poets, operating in the relatively free British-occupied Egypt, generated the spark that touched off the Pan-Arab movement. They coined new words or adapted old words for such new concepts as nationalism, patriotism, fatherland, and human rights. It was not long, however, before this nascent, fragile Pan-Arabism was fragmented in response to regional demands at the same time that it got confused with Pan-Islamism. The situation remains confused.

II

ONCE the political machinery is modernized the framework is set for transforming the economic and social aspects of life. Of these two the economic transformation is easier to achieve; it does not involve serious emotional strain or undue stress on ingrained loyalties. The typical nineteenth-century Arab society was rural and self-sufficient. Each small unit consumed in food and clothing only that which it produced. Tools for agriculture were primitive and easy to handle. Transportation was by animal and communication was by word of mouth. The twentieth-century farmer, however, began to use improved plows — perhaps tractors — and he introduced new crops and utilized chemicals for fertilizing the soil and fighting insects. His surplus product supplied the public market. The early craftsman likewise operated with hand tools and on a village level. The onslaught of technological products from Europe necessitated change. Village handicraft dwindled and native machine-made consumers' goods had to compete with foreign imports. The means of transportation were revolutionized by the introduction of motor vehicles and trains. The inevitable shift from rural to urban settlement proceeded at an accelerated pace. In North Africa and the Near East cities mushroomed where once there were only towns.

Under the impact of the West the social fabric of the community was being transformed at the same time as the economic life. The traditional Arab family was the extensive, patriarchal one, familiar since biblical days. It was generally rural and agrarian. The grandfather dominated the societal unit, held the property, and arranged for marriages. When the daughters or granddaughters were married they exchanged their ancestral relationships for those of their husbands' families. The family provided protection and economic security. It demanded undivided loyalty. In it solidarity, serenity, and pride in kinship were nurtured.

This type of organization was gradually replaced by the modern biological unit in which the marriageable couple choose each other, establish an independent residence, and often move to an urban settlement for commercial and industrial pursuits. Freedom in individual thought and action assumes a higher place in the scale of values than "belonging" and conforming. A concomitant of such social mobility is geographical mobility. Both involve nervous tension. As the woman lifts the veil and enters the economic life of the community, she faces new problems and temptations. Respect for old age, consideration for others' feelings, and other traditional values are discarded at a more rapid pace than new values are appropriated. Psychological conflicts arise. Crime, mental ailments, delinquency, and divorce increase. Westernization is far from being an unmixed blessing.

Of all forces affecting social change none are more potent than education — formal or informal. Until well into the nineteenth century the Arab system of education was conventional in pattern, reflecting a stagnant society. The mosque and church, rather than the state, supported and controlled it. Theology, scholasticism, and linguistics stood at the core of the curriculum. The student's role was passive rather than participatory. Physical science was not a favorite subject of study, and such words as "experimentation," "research," and "criticism" were not in the educators' vocabulary.

Egypt in the post-Napoleonic era led the way out of this impasse. Impressed by Europe's superiority in arms, technology, and economy, Egypt's viceroy Muhammad 'Ali (1805–48) embarked on a new procedure: he sent students to Europe to study and invited specialists from Europe to share their skills with Egypt. Between 1826 and 1834 more than a hundred students went abroad, mainly to France. In 1828 a French physician was invited to establish a school of medicine in Cairo, the first scientific institution in the entire area and still active. Following the example of Napoleon, who on his way had plundered an Arabic printing press from the Vatican for publicizing his "mission" in Egypt, Muhammad 'Ali founded in his capital a press that is still the official Egyptian one. Books were translated and published. Newspapers, learned societies, and schools made their appearance. The break with the past was under way. In their forty-year occupation the British made no attempt to update the educational system, although they did generate a congenial climate for the expression of free thought which attracted intellectuals, particularly from Lebanon.

Lebanon followed and soon outstripped Egypt in exposing itself to European influences. In fact, Lebanon had an earlier start but under entirely different circumstances. The tiny country had a preponderant Christian population — the only one in the Arab world — and a cool mountain climate — a rarity in the region. Catholic missionaries, mostly French, had operated there since the early seventeenth century. Schools served as their tools. In the nineteenth century their work was expanded, nuns were added, and boys' and girls' schools were no longer limited to towns. A printing press, Imprimerie Catholique, still one of the best equipped in that city of presses, was established (1853) in Beirut. French educational activity was crowned by the Université Saint-Joseph (1881), which has maintained a position of leadership to the present day.

The Protestant missions, mostly American, did not assume their role until the second quarter of the nineteenth century. They too chose to implant their ideas through education. Their press, founded (1835) in Beirut, began — in common with the Catholic press — with religious translations and tracts but later included scientific and literary publications. The Protestant educational institutions culminated in 1866 in Syrian Protestant College, now a private institution known as the American University of Beirut, the most influential American center of learning outside the United States. These two universities were responsible for introducing modern science and technology into western Asia. They, together with the Western-style native colleges that followed, attracted students from Syria, Iraq, and other neighboring lands. They made Beirut an international center of intellectual thought.

A distinctive feature of Lebanon, whose women are more fertile than its mountainous soil, is emigration. In the last decade of the nineteenth and the first of the twentieth century, migration, especially to the New World, assumed such proportions that people began to refer to two Lebanons: a resident and an emigrant one. By their correspondence, publications, and return visits Lebanese-Americans exercised a measure of Westernizing influence hard to assess. In one field, the literary, it is clear. Their poets and belletrists were the first to free themselves to a large extent from the shackles of the past and to blaze new trails in theme, vocabulary, and form. The new literary school they founded attracted followers throughout the Arab world.

With the increase of Western-educated men, a middle class of lawyers, physicians, teachers, engineers, and writers sandwiched itself between the two traditional layers of Arab society. Gradually members of this class inched their way upward into positions of leadership and influence, forcing members of the traditional upper class downward. Rigidity in the social structure yielded to mobility, and with it went mobility in finance and politics. It is this newly created middle class that is supplying the ranks of rulers and leaders in the modernized Arab states.

III

AS THE tidal wave of modernization, a worldwide phenomenon, crashed on the southern and eastern shores of the Mediterranean, most of the political, economic, social, and educational institutions were lost; only religious ones survived. Much of the opposition to Europeanization was prompted by a feeling on the part of the guardians of Islam that the intruding elements of the foreign culture might undermine not only the social structure of the host culture but the fundamentals of its faith and its ideal of the good life. Of the three Islams, Islam the state was the first to yield to the Western onslaught; Islam the religion the last. Even in religion one practice after another was discarded. Formal prayer five times a day, fasting during a whole month, paying alms, pilgrimage to the holy cities — all became in varying degrees incompatible with the demands of a modernized society. Secularization affected more practices than beliefs. Out of the debris of the traditional faith a solid core of dogmas remained intact. No modern Moslem thinker of stature has, so far, publicly challenged the oneness of God, the prophethood of Muhammad, the holiness of the Koran, the immortality of the soul, or the resurrection of the body. No one has preached that "God is dead."

One could well say there is no such thing as Arab culture or Western culture. All there is, is human culture, one stream with sources in the ancient Near East flowing westward to receive tributaries from Greece and Rome and later from Western Europe and the United States, then returning to the place from which it started. The world can view with gratitude Arab contributions of the past; it can look with hope to their contributions in the future.

A SELECT BIBLIOGRAPHY

Adams, C. C. *Islam and Modernism in Egypt*. London, 1933.

Afnan, Soheil N. *Avicenna: His Life and Works*. London, 1958.

Andrae, Tor. *Mohammad: The Man and His Faith*, tr. Theophil Menzel. New York, 1935.

Arberry, Arthur J. *Avicenna on Theology*. London, 1951.

———. *Revelation and Reason in Islam*. London and New York, 1957.

———. *Sufism*. London, 1950.

Arnold, Thomas W. *The Caliphate*. London, 1965.

———. *Painting in Islam*. Oxford, 1928.

———, and Alfred Guillaume, eds. *The Legacy of Islam*. Oxford, 1931.

Bell, Richard. *The Origin of Islam in Its Christian Environment*. London, 1926.

Berger, Morroe. *The Arab World Today*. New York, 1962.

Boer, T. J. de. *The History of Philosophy in Islam*, tr. Edward R. Jones. London, 1961.

Brockelmann, Carl. *History of the Islamic Peoples*, tr. Joel Carmichael and Moshe Perlmann. New York, 1947.

Chejne, Anwar G. *The Arabic Language: Its Role in History*. Minneapolis, 1969.

Ehwany, Ahmed F., el-. *Islamic Philosophy*. Cairo, 1957.

Ettinghausen, Richard. *Arab Painting*. Cleveland, 1962.

Farmer, Henry G. *Historical Facts for the Arabian Musical Instruments*. London, 1931.

Gabrieli, Francesco. *The Arab Revival*. New York, 1961.

Gardet, Louis. *Mohammedanism*, tr. William Burridge. New York, 1961.

Gibb, Hamilton A. R. *Arabic Literature*, 2nd ed. Oxford, 1963.

———. *Modern Trends in Islam*. Chicago, 1947.

———. *Mohammedanism: A Historical Survey*. Cambridge, Eng., 1953.

Holt, P. M. *Egypt and the Fertile Crescent*. Ithaca, N.Y., 1966.

Hourani, A. H. *Syria and Lebanon*. London, 1946.

Hyman, Arthur, and J. J. Walsh, eds. *Philosophy in the Middle Ages*. New York, 1967.

Jeffrey, Arthur, ed. *Islam: Muhammad and His Religion*. New York, 1958.
Kühnel, E. *Islamic Art and Architecture*, tr. Katherine Watson. Ithaca, N.Y., 1966.
Lammens, H. *Islam: Beliefs and Institutions*, tr. E. D. Ross. London, 1929.
Lenczowski, George. *The Middle East in World Affairs*, 3rd ed. Ithaca, N.Y., 1962.
Levy, Reuben. *A Baghdad Chronicle*. Cambridge, Eng., 1929.
Lewis, Bernard. *The Arabs in History*. London, 1950.
———. *The Origins of Isma'ilism*. Cambridge, Eng., 1940.
Lyall, Charles C. *Translations of Ancient Arabian Poetry*. New York, 1930.
Nasr, Seyyid Hossein. *Three Muslim Sages*. Cambridge, Mass., 1964.
Peters, F. E. *Aristotle and the Arabs*. New York, 1968.
Schacht, Joseph. *The Origins of Muhammadan Jurisprudence*. Oxford, 1950.
Sharif, M. M., ed. *A History of Muslim Philosophy*, vol. 1. Wiesbaden, 1963.
Sweetman, J. W. *Islam and Christian Theology*, pt. 1, vols. 1, 2. London, 1945–7.
Von Grunebaum, Gustave E. *Medieval Islam*, 2nd ed. Chicago, 1953.
Walzer, Richard. *Greek into Arabic: Essays on Islamic Philosophy*. Oxford, 1962.
Watt, W. Montgomery. *Free Will and Predestination in Early Islam*. Oxford, 1956.
———. *Islamic Philosophy and Theology*. Edinburgh, 1962.
———. *Muhammad at Mecca*. Oxford, 1933.
———. *Muhammad at Medina*. Oxford, 1958.
Wensinck, A. J. *The Muslim Creed*. Cambridge, Eng., 1932.
Winder, R. Bayly. *Saudi Arabia in the Nineteenth Century*. New York and London, 1965.
Wittek, Paul. *The Rise of the Ottoman Empire*. London, 1938.

Index

INDEX

'Amr ibn-al-'As, 21, 76, 80
Andalus, al-, 96, 143, 150
Andalusia, 96. *See also* Andalus, al-
Andalusian: forms, 150; school, 174
Ansar, 14, 143. *See also* Supporters
'Antar, 140–1, 142
'Antarah, 140. *See also* 'Antar
Apostles' Creed, 39
Aqsa Mosque, al-, 34
Aquinas, Thomas, 130, 136
Arab: states, 3, 10, 176, 182; nation, 15, 24; intellectualism, 65; mercenaries, 76; historians, 77, 78, 80, 81; empire, 78; history, 82; world, 92, 153, 159; chroniclers, 100; caliphate, 102; culture, 106, 124; science, 112; traders, 114; alchemists, 120; physicians, 120; philosophy, 130, 131, 136, 173; philosophers, 136; chivalry, 141; ideals, 142; poetry, 148; poets, 154, 155, 166, 169; decoration, 162; painter, 163; sculpture, 163, 177, 183; neighbors, 165; art, 166; artist, 166; music, 171; sources, 172; contributions, 175; society, 176, 182; lands, 177, 178; world, 181; contributions, 183
Arab East, 151, 177
Arab Islam, 178
Arab Moslem: influence, 151
'Arabi, ibn-, 61–3, 132
Arabia: 2, 42, 72, 73, 106, 178; polytheism in, 18; pilgrimage in, 37; pre-Islamic, 39; isolated, 47; heathen, 141; music in, 168–9
Arabian: peninsula, 3, 39, 77, 79; tribes, 9, 77, 84, 87; warfare, 16; origins, 92; blood, 122; stories, 154; history, 171
Arabian Nights, 154–5
Arabianism, 77
Arabians: 3, 25, 48, 78, 79, 87, 107; contacts with, 20; control of, 73; idols of, 163
Arabic: 106–7, 138; language, 9, 26, 48, 82, 156; prose in, 27; literature, 27, 63, 73, 98, 108, 138, 142, 144, 151, 168; translations into, 91–2, 133, 135; numerals, 110; poetry, 139; style, 151; letters, 167; writing, 167, 168; script, 168; tradition, 171; music, 172, 174; press, 181
Arabic-Islamic: culture, 24
Arabic-Spanish: music, 174
Arabism, 149

Arabization, 18, 82
Arabs: 62, 82, 87, 129, 166, 172; medieval, 25, 39; threaten Europe, 40; as transmitters, 137; as poets, 148; mind of, 178
Aramaic, 33
Aristotelian: logic, 44, 121, 122; views, 123; system, 125
Aristotelianism, 130, 134
Aristotle, 92, 122–3, 125, 128, 130, 134, 172, 173
Armenia, 76
Armenian: mercenaries, 76
Ash'ari, al-, 50
Ash'arite: theology, 50
Ash'arites, 50
Asia: 3, 72, 77, 82; central, 81, 98; western, 100, 119, 133
Asia Minor, 62, 98, 100
Asian: languages, 152
Assassin: order, 101
Assyria, 159
Athens, 92, 108, 122
Athir, ibn-al-, 101
Atlantic, 82, 90
Avenpace, 173
Averroes, 135, 136. *See also* Rushd, ibn-
Averroism, 135, 136
Avicenna, 58, 129, 130. *See also* Sina, ibn-
Azhar, al-, 95
'Aziz, al-, 96

Babylon (in Egypt), 76
Babylonian, 111
Babylonians, 35–6, 107
Bacon, Roger, 130
Badr, 16
Baghdad: 3, 4, 26, 44, 52, 59, 61, 64, 67, 68, 97, 98, 100, 141, 143, 146, 147; capital, 88–9, 92; caliphate, 94; spared, 101, 108, 111, 112; hospital in, 115; philosophy in, 122, 123, 124, 129, 131, 137; cafés of, 141; court, 170; physicians in, 172; music in, 174
Baghdadis, 97, 101
Bahira, 19
Bahrayn, 22
Bajjah, ibn-, 173
Bakr, abu- (caliph), 12, 14, 73, 76, 78, 79
Baktra, 101. *See also* Balkh
Balkans, 100
Balkh, 101, 129

189

190

Dead Sea, 21, 161
Deborah, 10
Decalogue, 137
Deneb, 120
Deuteronomy, 41
Dhimmis (covenant people), 79, 84
Dioscorides, 92, 119
Dome of the Rock, 82, 159–60
Druzes, 51
Druzism, 96
Duns Scotus, John, 130

East, 109, 110, 112, 125, 147, 148, 173, 177
East Roman Empire, 2, 72
Eastern: caliphate, 122; influence, 150; stories, 154; tales, 155
Eastern Christians, 78
Eastern Islam, 82, 158
Egypt, 39, 43, 72, 76, 78, 80, 86, 98, 100, 107, 110, 112, 166, 171, 178, 181
Egyptian: origins, 92; sources, 154; craftsmen, 158
Egyptians, 36, 77, 108, 163
Elijah, 35
Emigrants, 14
Empedocles, 132
England, 177
English: history, 84; translation, 108; language, 151; literature, 155
Enoch, 34
Epistles, 19
Europe, 3, 40, 92, 112, 119, 124, 133, 150, 177, 180, 181
European: territory, 82; universities, 136; literatures, 138; languages, 152, 174; codes, 178; influences, 181
Europeanization, 183
Europeans, 111, 154, 174
Exodus, 41

Faqih, ibn-al-, 158
Farabi, al-, 124–5, 151, 172
Faraj ben-Salim, 116
Fatimah (Muhammad's daughter), 46, 51
Fatimid: caliphate, 96; empire, 96
Fatimid Baghdad, 96
Fatimids, 96, 98
Fazari, al-, 110
Fertile Crescent, 4, 77, 121, 166
Fiqh (Islamic law), 44

Firdawsi, 155
First Crusade, 100
France, 84, 141, 150, 151, 177, 178, 181
Frankish army, 84
Franks, 25, 95
Frederick II of Sicily, 136
French: educational activity, 181; physician, 181
Friday (day of prayer), 18, 34
Fustat, al-, 78, 96

Gabirol, ben-, 132
Gabriel (angel), 8, 31, 38, 126
Galen, 92, 115
Galenic tradition, 117
Galland, 154
Gaza, 44
Geber, 119
Gentile Christianity, 42
Georgia, 101
Gerard of Cremona, 110–1, 113, 118, 124
Geronimo Cardono, 124
Ghanim, 142
Ghassan, 169
Ghassanids, 19
Ghaznawid, 152
Ghazzah, 44
Ghazzali, al-, 50, 66–9, 131, 173, 176
Gibbon, 84
God: 8, 9, 10, 11, 13, 20, 55–8, 127–8; word of, 26, 31, 168; attributes of, 30; works of, 31; oneness of, 33, 183; obligations to, 42; almightiness of, 48; communion with, 54; as creator, 123, 164; existence of, 125–6, 130, 136; knowledge of, 132. *See also* Allah
Gomorrah, 34
Gospels, 19
Granada, 95, 132, 162
Great Britain, 178
Greece, 183
Greek: 110, 130; law, 41; philosophy, 44, 47–8, 68; language, 47, 79, 91; fire, 80; medicine, 115; philosophy, 121; thought, 122; science, 128; elements, 129; sources, 154; music, 171–2, 173
Greeks, 41, 108, 121, 123, 172
Guadalquivir, 95

Hadith (tradition): 42–3; collection of, 33, 34; Prophetic, 44; Sunnite, 46
Hafiz, 62

44, 46–7; mind, 48; theology, 50; piety, 53, 68; civilization, 107; revelation, 123; buildings, 158; art, 159, 165; culture, 172, 176
Islamization, 77
Isma'il (imam), 51–2
Isma'il (son of Abraham), 38
Isma'ilis, 51
Isma'ilism, 51
Israeli-Arab outbreaks, 35
Italian cities, 96
Italy, 40, 150

Jabir ibn-Hayyan, 119
Jacob, 9
Jaffa, 94
Jami, 62
Jamil al-'Udhri, 144
Jarir, 144
Java, 64
Jehovah, 41. See also God
Jeremiah, 10
Jerusalem: 17, 26, 34, 37, 67, 81, 95; rendezvous at, 35; religious capital, 92; prayer toward, 157; sanctuary in, 158
Jesus, 9, 11, 19, 20, 40, 125, 163
Jewish: tribes, 5, 18; neighbors, 17; settlements, 20; practice, 36; thinking, 69; philosophy, 136; sources, 154
Jewish Sabbath, 34
Jewish Wailing Wall, 35
Jews: 5, 11, 16, 32, 106; break with, 17; expulsion of, 18; hostility of, 20; tolerated, 79. See also Judaism
Jiddah, 157
Jilani, al-, 64
Jili, al-, 64
John of Damascus, 47, 76
John of Halifax, 110
John of Seville, 113
John the Baptist, 11, 158
John the Divine, 26
Jordan (river), 76, 160
Jordan (state), 102
Judaeo-Christian: tradition, 31; institution, 35; ideas, 52
Judaism: 2, 8, 15, 17, 18; adherents of, 84
Jupiter, 158
Justinian, 160

Kaabah: 11, 12, 17, 18, 140; idols in, 22; arrows in, 30; founder of, 37, 156–7; deity of, 163; pilgrimage to, 169
Ka'bah, al-, 11
Kairouan, 81. See also Qayrawan, al-
Kalam (scholastic theology), 50
Kalbi, ibn-al-, 163
Khadijah, 12, 13
Khaldun, ibn-, 148, 176
Khalid al-Barmaki, 88
Khalid ibn-al-Walid, 21, 73, 76
Khaybar, 18, 20
Khirbat al-Mafjar, 160–1
Khumarawayh, 164
Khurasan, 101, 171
Khurasani, al-, 85, 87
Khwarizm, 100
Khwarizmi al-, 91, 109–11, 112–3, 176
Kiblah (direction of prayer), 18, 37
Kindah, 122
Kindi, al-, 113, 115, 122–5, 126, 129, 134, 136, 151, 172
Konia, 62
Konieh, 62
Koran: 4, 11, 16, 23, 27–33, 126, 151; revelation of, 8; language of, 9; dictated, 26; character of, 39; recorded in, 42; creation of, 49; dogma of, 49; consecrated in, 121; knowledge of, 125; idols in, 163; on monotheism, 164; copyists of, 168; on music, 169; reciting of, 173; holiness of, 183
Kufah: 59, 78, 85–6, 88, 122, 144, 146, 153; mosque of, 87
Kufic, 168

La Fontaine, Jean de, 91
Lakhmids, 19
Lane, E. William, 154
Latin: language, 28, 108; translation into, 110, 111, 112, 113, 115–6, 118, 120, 124, 129–30, 152
Latin West, 137
Latins, 133
Layla, 144
Lebanese, 179
Lebanese-Americans, 182
Lebanon, 51, 96, 107, 178, 181–2
Leonardo Fibonacci, 111
Leviticus, 41
Libya, 65, 81
Logos, 26, 62
London, 84
Luqman, 121

nation, 98, 129; sources, 154; tales, 155; language, 177
Turkish Moslems, 179
Turks, 39, 129, 166, 177
Tus, 66
Tutili, al-, 150
Twelvers, 51–2
Tyre, 91, 122, 165

'Ubaydullah al-Mahdi, 96
Uhud, 16–7
'Ukaz, 140, 143, 169
'Uman, 22
'Umar (Medina caliph), 13, 14, 21, 76, 78, 79, 82, 159
'Umar II, 144
'Umar al-Khayyam, 63–4, 111
'Umar ibn-abi-Rabi'ah, 144
Umayyad: clan, 12; vigilance, 13; court, 47; dynasty, 79; house, 84; cause, 85; regime, 87, 88; caliphs, 89, 92, 94, 96, 149; caliphate in Spain, 132; period, 143; architecture, 161; dynasty in Spain, 161
Umayyad Mosque, 67, 82, 158
Umayyads: 52, 149, 160; oppose Muhammad, 13; leadership of, 15; as usurpers, 170
Ummah (religious community), 42
United States, 182, 183
Université Saint-Joseph, 181
Urdu: literature, 138, 142
'Uthman ibn-'Affan, 79
'Uzza, al-, 24, 163

Vatican, 181
Venice, 119, 136

Wahhabis, 47

Walid, al-, 82, 85, 158, 161
Walladah, 149–50
West, 66, 109, 110, 125, 132, 136, 154, 163, 174, 177, 180
Western: historians, 84; culture, 130, 175, 183; importation, 178; onslaught, 183
Western Europe, 183
Western European, 92, 95, 131, 177, 179
Western Islam, 95, 133
Western Moslems, 81
Westerners, 167
Word of Allah, 45, 49, 56
World War I, 16, 178
World War II, 178

Yahweh, 26. See also God
Yaman, 5, 39, 96
Yaqut, 114
Yarmuk, 76
Yathrib, 3, 13. See also Medina
Yazdagird, 77
Yazid, 80, 81, 170
Yaziji, al-, 153
Yusuf, abu-Ya'qub, 133–4

Zacharias, 11
Zahra', al-, 95, 149, 164
Zahrawi, al-, 118–9
Zakah (alms), 22, 35
Zamzam, 12, 38, 163
Zarqali, al-, 113
Zayd, 18
Zaydun, ibn-, 149–50
Zechariah, 10
Ziryab, 174
Zoroastrian, 56
Zubaydah, 90